LOST VOICES OF THE
LONDON TRAMS

LOST VOICES OF THE
LONDON TRAMS

....

MICHAEL H.C. BAKER

First published 2014

ISBN 978 0 7110 3685 7

Published by Ian Allan Publishing Ltd, Hersham, Surrey, KT12 4RG

Printed in China

Visit the Ian Allan Publishing website at
www.ianallanpublishing.com

Photographs
Unless otherwise credited, photographs are by the author or from the author's collection.

For my best friend, Maeve

Front cover: The lazy days of a scene familiar in inner south-east London for some 50 years as an ex-London County Council 'E3' and a former East Ham Corporation 'E1' head through Camberwell on their respective ways to the West End and the City in the summer of 1952. *Rev A. W. V. Mace*

Back cover: An animated scene in Brixton in the late 1930s with at least three trams negotiating for space with ST-type buses, cars, cyclists and pedestrians. *London Transport*

Title page: A former Croydon Corporation E1 heads through Streatham on its way from Purley to the Embankment c1949 *F.G.Reynolds*

CONTENTS

INTRODUCTION

A picture which frightened the life out of the author, who, for years afterwards, as a child in wartime South London, had nightmares about being caught in such an incident. A bomb landed smack on a railway bridge in Blackfriars Road on 25 October 1940, penetrating it and exploding on the two 'E1s' beneath, crowded with passengers. The death toll, needless to say, was considerable. *B. J. Cross Collection/Online Transport Archive*

It would be overstating the case, considerably, to claim that for the first 14 years of my life the tram occupied my thoughts for a considerable part of the day and my dreams at night. Had this been so, your reaction would, hopefully, be to urge me to 'Get a life'. Nevertheless – ah, here we go – trams and I had a close relationship. I rejoiced in just about all forms of transport, from the high pram which was my first and which I don't remember, through the grey/green-coloured push chair, which I do, a Mickey Mouse tricycle which I soon came

to despise as being a symbol of my distant infancy, the wooden cart which my father constructed, which I used to wheel around the neighbourhood and upon which I inscribed the legend 'Morris 8', and, of course, to any tram, bus or train which I encountered.

To one growing up in Thornton Heath between 1937 and 1951 the tram was the most normal and most favoured form of transport, and so it remained until some misguided soul at 55 Broadway decided enough was enough and took my tram away on 7 April 1951. I was just entering

Above: London can sometimes give the appearance – and not by chance – of being a surprisingly leafy city, as demonstrated by this scene on the Embankment, featuring a rehabilitated 'E1' and a 'Feltham' going about their business on a sunny September day in 1948. *B. T. Cooke/B. J. Cross Collection*

Above: A rehabilitated 'E1' on its way to West Norwood follows an Austin taxi of c1936 vintage as a gent on a bicycle of indeterminate age offers his threepenny-worth to the group ranging from ladies out shopping to a schoolgirl, discussing what to do about the spot of bother into which STL2405 seems to have got itself on a sunny day in Camberwell c1947.

Above: Former Croydon 'E1' No 381 undergoing maintenance at Purley depot in October 1950. *Grenville Williams*

The 'misguided soul' intent on removing the tram from streets of London was a collective body, but there was one individual who did as much as any to achieve this end – Frank Pick. As it happens, the more research I do into Frank Pick the more he becomes one of my all-time heroes, a towering genius who took Crystal Palace into the Premier League, was Wallis Simpson's first choice for her third husband, rode a bicycle on a tightrope across the English Channel and persuaded Ian Paisley to stand for Pope. Well, perhaps he didn't actually achieve all that, but I'm sure he could have, if only he hadn't been fully occupied in turning London Transport into the most progressive urban transport authority in the world, bar none. Yet even towering geniuses can possess Achilles' heels, and in a paper he wrote in 1920, when London's tram network was almost (although not entirely) complete, Pick asserted that 'The street railway is an intermediate solution good until a more highly specialized scheme of transport facilities is wanted … this explains why London cannot now ever be a tramway city. The tram has gone by the time the phase is past.' He it was who was Managing Director of London Transport when, in 1935, the decision was made to abandon the tram. But I forgive him; as we shall see later on.

Long after my last ride on a London tram I used to have dreams of coming across lost corners of suburbia where, at the last moment, there had been a reprieve, and 'E1s' and 'E3s' still plied their trade. This was not

my teens, a period when the certainties of childhood are beginning to fracture, an experience both exhilarating and terrifying, to say nothing of what it does to parents. I wouldn't wish the reader to imagine for one moment that the disappearance of routes 16, 18 and 42 was the most traumatic happening of my adolescence, but it certainly contributed to the realisation that my world was changing. I use the word 'tram' collectively, for on that spring day in April the powers that be actually removed some 70 cars which hitherto were allocated to Purley and Telford Avenue depots to work the routes which passed the top of our road during the morning and evening rush hours; during the rest of the day the number required was 43. My earliest perception was that there were two types of tram – the long tram and the short tram. Nothing that I subsequently learned contradicted this, but it needed refining. There was just one variety of the former, the 'Feltham', and many of the latter, which was everything else (of which more anon).

Above: One of Milan's famous '1500'-class ('Peter Witt') trams – of which 502 were built, the first in 1927 – still in service in 2001.

such a total fantasy, for many cities worldwide which started to removed their tram or streetcar networks realised at some point in the process that they had made a mistake, and stopped the slaughter. Thus on my first visit to Italy in 1966, when I was amazed to discover in Milan that big single-deckers dating back to the 1920s were still an integral part of the public-transport scene, one would also come across abandoned sections of line, crossings which led nowhere and poles supporting sections of partly dismantled overhead, and as I travelled further afield, through Switzerland, Austria, Germany, then Scandinavia, Russia, eastwards across the Bosphorus into Asia and, later still, across the Atlantic, this became

a familiar situation, sometimes the trams rather elderly and decrepit but soldiering on, elsewhere the fleets beginning to be renewed with smooth, almost silent (except for the so-familiar clatter at crossings) articulated cars, until, some three decades after London's last tram had met its fiery end at Penhall Road, Charlton, in January 1953, there began a wholesale, worldwide renaissance of the tram, which would – miraculously and still slightly unbelievably – bring it back to the streets of my home town.

After London had taken away my trams and before venturing abroad 'proper' I did get to visit a few later survivors in the British Isles, three of which were halfway to being abroad. One was in Wales, another in Scotland and the third in Ireland, of which the last actually a near miss. In May 1959 I had hitch-hiked to South Wales and discovered that the line from Swansea along the coast to The Mumbles was still intact and operated by massive, 106-seat Brush-built double-deckers, which had something of the air of the 'Feltham' about them and were of similar vintage (1929); they ceased to run two years later, and, sadly, all that survives is just one end of

Above: Two small single-deck cars make their way past a pair of Mercedes and other traffic in Street Called Straight – the very one along which St Paul walked – in Damascus in October 1966, a year before the tramway closed down. It had opened in 1907, the first in the Ottoman Empire.

Left: A long-disused section of track in Warsaw in June 2012. In the far distance it is just possible to see a tram turning to the right on a still-extant section.

Left: No 720, one of Blackpool Corporation's streamlined, high-capacity 'Balloon' trams of 1934, heading north towards Fleetwood on reserved track.

Opposite: Liverpool 'Baby Grand' No 266 of 1938 in Lime Street on 26 August 1957, a month before the end of Liverpool's trams.

one of these magnificent cars, No 7. In those days hitch-hiking was virtually the standard means of travel for impecunious students, and this was how I got to Scotland the following summer. Glasgow still had a remarkable number of trams at work, and I stood in Argyle Street by Central station, marvelling at the procession – not just of the streamlined 'Coronations' and 'Cunarders' but the much older 'Kilmarnock Bogies' and the archaic 'Standards', beside which a London 'E1' would have looked positively modern. There were, incidentally, around 1,000 of each. That summer I also made my first visit to Ireland. It proving impossible to hitch-hike across the Irish Sea, I had to fork out hard-earned, working-on-the-buildings holiday money, and on a trip from Dublin to Howth found I had missed out on a tram ride up to the summit by just four months, a number of the cars being still in the depot at Sutton.

It was the Liverpool system I knew best. I would eventually study and live on Merseyside in the mid-1960s, when there were still stretches of tram track visible in the cobbles, but the trams themselves disappeared on 14 September 1957. As late as 1955 I came across a number of the early-1930s 'Cabin Cars' and 'Marks Bogies' (which looked not unlike the LCC's No 1) laid up

in Edge Lane Works, leaving the final routes to be worked by the late-1930s streamlined four-wheel 'Baby Grands' and the bogied 'Green Goddesses'. I say late 1930s, but rather like London's 'prewar' RTs the final Liverpool tram, a 'Baby Grand', did not enter service until October 1942. On my first visit, although I was pretty sure I'd read somewhere that the Liverpool trams was doomed, there seemed to be so many working so many routes in Lime Street and down at the Pier Head – Liverpool's equivalent of London's Embankment— that I went along to the head office in Dale Street to ask if it was really true they would shortly be gone. 'It is,' came the grim-faced reply.

Then, of course, there was – and is – Blackpool. To take a ride down the main street of a town (Fleetwood, to be precise) in a tram in the UK in the mid-1950s and know that its future was assured was an experience to be savoured. When the family came up to visit me in Southport in the autumn of 1964 we drove to Blackpool for the Illuminations. Naturally enough it rained, which at least added to the atmosphere, with the lights glistening in the puddles, but we had to wait at the tram stop by the tower for what seemed like an eternity before finding space as one packed tram followed closely behind another.

1

AROUND THE POND

Inside Thornton Heath depot c1935. From left to right are 'E1s' Nos 1002 (route 42) and 1417 (30), former Croydon Corporation 'E1' No 375 (16) and a newly rehabilitated 'E1' (42). No 1002 was scrapped at the other former Croydon Corporation depot at Purley in March 1946, its lower saloon being sold off, whilst 1417 was put into store, without ever being fitted with windscreens, for the duration of the war and was destroyed in a fire at Hampstead depot on 1 October 1946. No 397, fitted with windscreens in June 1939, lasted until October 1951. *London Transport*

I was brought up at No 8 Broughton Road in Thornton Heath. At the top end of our road was the London Road, along which tram routes 16, 18 and 42, several bus routes and, once the war was over, five Green Line routes plied their trade. At the other end was the A23, the main London–Brighton road (which the London Road had once been), along which worked bus route 115 – and also, once the war was over, Southdown Leyland Tiger coaches, in their beautiful two shades of green, on their way to and from Brighton, Eastbourne and other Sussex seaside towns. These would be joined at summer weekends by all manner of vehicles, ranging from the AECs, Leylands, Dennises and Bedfords of such well-known companies as Orange, Grey-Green and Banfields to ancient Tilling-Stevens, Gilfords and the like belonging to small, one-man businesses.

Along the London Road going north towards Thornton Heath Pond was Whitehall Road, and beyond that Thornton Heath tram depot. Here I spent many happy hours – not inside (goodness no, although I would have loved to venture within) but on the pavement outside, beside the inspector who had very nearly the most prestigious and enviable job in the world, that of controlling the points, sending the 42s around the sharp bend into Brigstock Road or the 16s and 18s straight on towards London. He was luckier than many such pointsmen, for when it rained he, unlike them, had a canvas shelter into which he could retire. He was positioned outside a gloomy-looking old red-brick house which rejoiced in the name of Brigstock Villa. It had been the headquarters of Croydon Corporation Tramways (until the latter's absorption into London Transport in 1933), which status must once have lent it a certain air, but by my time it was living in reduced circumstances. Presumably it served some administrative purpose, but it held no interest for me, and by the time, many decades later, I began to make enquires it was long gone, and there was no one around who could enlighten me. The tramway had reached Thornton Heath Pond in 1879, a horse-operated line to/from West Croydon opening on 3 October

Above: The author with his mother and a donkey (the latter employed in hauling the knife-sharpener's vehicle) outside the family home in Broughton Road, Thornton Heath, in 1938. It is just possible to discern at the top of the road one of the poles supporting the overhead for the 16, 18 and 42 tram routes.

that year. With electrification in 1901 the depot at Thornton Heath was 'reconstructed', but Brigstock Villa, also dating from 1879, was left unmolested, its architectural style, such as it was, being typical of that era.

We ought before we go any further to distinguish between Thornton Heath and Thornton Heath Pond. The latter had existed for centuries and gave its name to the district. Being on the main road between London and the Sussex coast, it attracted a variety of citizens, good and bad, amongst the latter being Dick Turpin, no less, who for a time lived in a cottage there, apparently with his Aunty; what she thought of his profession is not recorded. He was not the only villain in the locality; indeed there were so many of them that one of the earliest public amenities, other than the pond, was a set of gallows, which continued to serve the bad end of the populace well into the 18th century – and provide grisly entertainment for the rest. The pond offered refreshment for the horses of the colliers on their way along Colliers Wood Lane to the Great North Wood – Norwood – which from the late 1850s, thanks to Prince Albert and Joseph Paxton, became better known as Crystal Palace. This wood was used in the making of charcoal, a product for which the area was renowned; the smoke from burning charcoal was said to be excellent for the complexion, and consequently the residents of the district were famed for their smooth skins. Certainly when, at the age of four, I began my education at Rosedene School for Girls, Preparatory for Boys, a few hundred yards from the pond, I fell in love (when not peering out of the window to try to record the numbers of passing trams) with Pamela, the 15-year-old Senior Girl, and no doubt her glowing complexion was part of her allure.

Thornton Heath proper really was no more than uninhabited heathland until the London, Brighton & South Coast Railway built its line from Clapham Junction to Croydon in the early 1860s and opened a station at Thornton Heath in 1862. Selhurst station, the next one down the line towards Croydon and which opened in

Right: A rare view of a rehabilitated 'E1', No 1001, without windscreens, at the back of Thornton Heath depot shortly after being rebuilt in the autumn of 1934. It beggars belief that London Transport could have been so mean-spirited as to go to the length of upgrading a tram and yet leaving it without windscreens. In the event poor old No 1001 was a lame duck, retaining its 42hp motors instead of receiving 60hp motors, as were fitted to other 'E1s'. In 1937 it was sent north to Stamford Hill, eventually becoming the first 'rehab' to be withdrawn, from Leyton depot, in June 1939, and being broken up within a month.

Below: 'E3' No 1911 of Thornton Heath depot on 7 January 1951, heading past Broad Green towards Mayday Road and then the Pond, where it will swing eastwards up Brigstock Road to the 42 terminus at the end of Thornton Heath High Street. Immediately beyond is another 'E3', with much greater ambitions, bound for the Embankment. The author often used to wonder what was contained in the vaguely art-deco tower of the Croydon Automobile Co (this being an area not overburdened with interesting architectural features) and was rather disappointed to discover, as he watched it being demolished some years later, that it was merely an empty advertising structure. *J. H. Meredith*

Above: Ex-Croydon 'E1' No 388 about to turn out of Brigstock Road, opposite Thornton Heath depot, and head down the London Road to Croydon *c*1949. In the distance are the Norwood (formerly Northwood) Heights, upon which stood the Crystal Palace. *Ian Allan Library*

Above: East Croydon station shortly after trams commenced running, in January 1902. Serving Addiscombe, the route was by the 1920s becoming something of a burden to the local authority, and on 29 March 1927 it was abandoned, London General buses taking over.

Above: An Edwardian estate agent's poster featuring the newly introduced trams as an incentive to purchase a handsome villa near East Croydon.

1865, was originally named Colliers Water Lane. Once these two stations appeared the area began to develop: rows of shops lined the High Street, public baths were opened, and from 1881 it was served by trams, so that by the early 20th century, when those from outside the borough thought of Thornton Heath (which may not have been all that often), it was of the area around the High Street rather than the pond – none of which prevent us 'Pondites' from regarding our bit of what had in 1883 become the County Borough of Croydon as superior to that around the High Street.

My grandparents and their three boys moved into Broughton Road at the dawn of the 20th century; we have a picture taken at the time looking down it from the London Road, and at the far end is the countryside. Although Grandad had a good job (he was a chartered accountant) the house was rented, as were most in the district; it was not until the early

Above: The author's grandparents, Henry and Harriet Baker, around the time they moved to Thornton Heath in 1905.

1960s that Dad finally bought it, not long before the family headed off down the Brighton Road for good, to Sussex. Married life for my grandparents had begun in Clapham; later they moved to Hampstead, and later still from there back to Clapham before the final move south. Uncle Harry, born in 1887 and the oldest of the boys, used to tell me of watching the building of the Great Central Railway line, which passed through Hampstead on its way to Marylebone and opened in 1899.

It was towards the end of the 19th century that the area around Thornton Heath Pond began to develop, builders being encouraged by the arrival of the railway and the trams, so that it became quite possible, if one were sufficiently well-off, to commute to the City (which Grandad did, to Queen Victoria Street, where he worked for a firm of clothing importers until a few weeks before his death in 1936 at the age of 81). However, no-one made a fortune out of property in Thornton Heath.

Above: The view down Broughton Road, Thornton Heath, from London Road, just before work began on erecting the overhead and re-laying the track in the spring of 1901, in readiness for electrification. Broughton Road is not yet complete, there being open country at the far end.

Above: A quarter to eleven on an Edwardian morning in Clapham, looking south towards the Common – a picture taken around the time the author's grandparents moved from here to Thornton Heath. Bound for Tooting is tram No 457, one of the original 'E'-class cars of 1906 sent new to Clapham depot, where it lived until withdrawn by London Transport in the late 1930s. Aside from the older 'A'-class four-wheeler in the distance it is the only mechanically propelled vehicle in evidence.

The Thornton Heath & District Building Society set itself up business in 1881, bought farmland around the pond … and went bankrupt a year later. Later that decade, in a report to a Parliamentary select committee, a landowner complained: 'I had an opportunity to buy [seven acres of] land close to Thornton Heath station. Of course it brings me no income at all.' Land was often overvalued, and several speculative builders went out of business because they could not let their properties.

Superior persons could be very patronising and sniffy about property in the Thornton Heath area. The great Nikolaus Pevsner, who although he is owed much gratitude for his work in cataloguing the buildings of

Britain, was prone to expressing some rather odd opinions, among them that 'Thornton Heath has a desperate kind of mid-nineteenth-century character' (a remark which, when analysed, doesn't actually make any sense), whilst in 1976 D. Olsen, writing of 'the slopes of the Norwood hills',

Below: Thornton Heath Pond c1890. Just out of view, behind the camera, was the terminus of the horse trams which had commenced running as far as North End (Croydon's principal shopping thoroughfare and the main road to Brighton) on 9 October 1879.

expressed the view that 'the mass-produced villas failed ludicrously to be baronial castles or ducal hunting lodges' – which doubtless true but is also irrelevant, as there is nothing to indicate that any designer of these rather handsome villas (those that haven't been replaced by dull, bland, low-rise flats) ever intended that they should be.

I got to be very familiar with our locality, partly because the journey to Winterbourne Primary School, which I attended from January 1946 until July 1948, took in a fair bit of the area north of the pond and partly because during holiday time I used to assist the milkman on his round. The school was actually in Norbury and had a London postal address, although it fell under the ægis of the Croydon Education Committee. Before we leave the subject of milk, you need to know that in the early days of my employment as an apprentice milkman the float was horse-drawn – which was excellent, for when the round was completed I would join the captain of our conveyance up aloft, feeling very superior and almost high enough to see into the upper decks of trams (which despite their racket had no effect on the equanimity of the horses) and buses proceeding along the London Road, whence we turned up Mayday Road to the stables in Bensham Lane. Unfortunately progress ultimately intervened, and the United Dairies horses were pensioned off, the float being replaced by a pootling little electric affair which the milkman controlled by walking in front holding a lever whilst I trailed behind.

Above: A postcard view of Thornton Heath station in the early 1900s, featuring one of the original Corporation four-wheel Milnes & Co trams of 1901. The Milnes factory was at Hadley, in Shropshire, a county which today one thinks of as deeply rural – well, the writer does, having spent his childhood holidays roaming its fields and farmyards – but which was the cradle of the Industrial Revolution. The rather grand station building is almost brand-new, having been constructed in 1903 when the tracks passing beneath it were quadrupled.

As far as United Dairies was concerned, if the firm even knew of my existence (which it probably didn't, as nine-year-olds were not supposed to be employed), my name was Brian. The milkman always addressed me thus, and although I tried initially to persuade him otherwise it never seemed to sink in, so after a while I gave up, and for the rest of my time in his employ I answered to

Left: Former Croydon Corporation No 3, renumbered 347 by London Transport but retaining its old livery, has reached the Crystal Palace terminus at the top of Anerley Hill, its indicator already showing 'West Croydon'. It would shortly be withdrawn and broken up, in February 1936 to be precise, when trolleybuses take over; with their smooth, fully enclosed bodywork, comfortable upholstered seats and near-silent progress these magnificent vehicles must have seemed, to the inhabitants of Upper and South Norwood, Crystal Palace supporters and other discerning clients, like something from the space age. The contrast with the RTs, which in turn replaced the trolleybuses in 1959, was almost minimal by comparison. Truth to tell, apart from the original 'Diddlers', no London trolleybus ever seemed old-fashioned.

'Brian'; quite a popular name then, less so now. I suppose it was better than being called Wayne, which might have been my lot generations later. (There goes the Wayne market, unless the publishers excise this reference.)

The journey to Winterbourne Primary School took me along London Road, or rather, if walking, along the alleyways behind it. These alleyways were bewitching places, or so the group of us who proceeded along them, keeping together for mutual protection, were convinced, for there were always several rather scruffy-looking delivery vans, lacking any sign of ownership, parked up. These, there was no doubt, belonged to gangs of thieves, waiting until the coast was clear to rob the shops which fronted the London Road. We could never understand why these robberies did not get reported in the local paper, the *Croydon Advertiser*; many years later my first proper job was as a trainee reporter on that august organ, and I kick myself that I never thought to check back to see just why. Anyone who suggests that we were unduly influenced by those stirring crime fighters, Dick Barton, Jock and Snowy, to whom we faithfully tuned in on the Light Programme at a quarter to seven each evening, Monday to Friday, is jumping to altogether unwarranted conclusions, although it is an inescapable fact that when *The Archers* took Dick Barton's place BBC radio drama began to descend a slippery slope from which it has never recovered. Where are my Paul Temple and PC49 of long ago?

Occasionally I would cycle to school and one day in early July 1948 the headmaster, Mr Frame, wandered

Above: One of the 'B1'-type short-wheelbase trolleybuses working the 654 route, which took over from the Crystal Palace and Sutton trams, near the Crystal Palace football ground, South Norwood, in 1955.

into our class and asked if anyone had a bike in school. My hand shot up. Did I know the locality of various nearby other primary schools? I assured him I did, at which he handed me several envelopes with the words: 'Pop on your bike and deliver these for me, will you? They're rather important.' If this wasn't the proudest moment of my two and a half years at Winterbourne Primary School, it comes very close to it. I had passed the Eleven Plus, there was only a week or so to go before the summer holidays, and no doubt Mr Frame felt I would be perfectly usefully employed – which of course I was. The point of the story is that my ride involved negotiating several sets of tram lines, always a potential hazard for cyclists, but both parents and head teacher clearly had no qualms about my dealing with these. Stan Collins, possibly the only London tram driver to have his memoirs published, thought little of the tracks in Thornton Heath and

Left: An ex-Croydon Corporation 'E1' makes its way along Thornton Heath High Street c1950, having just begun its 16-minute journey to the 'Greyhound', Croydon.

Left: Former Croydon 'E1' No 384 working Croydon local route 42 waits for a lorry to cross from Whitehorse Lane into Thornton Heath High Street before completing the remaining few yards of its journey c1950. There was a time when tracks extended the length of Whitehorse Road, the continuation of the High Street, and back to central Croydon, and until 1959 it remained possible to travel by electric propulsion further along Whitehorse Road on the 654 trolleybus which replaced the Crystal Palace–Croydon tram route in 1935. More than half a century later, Tramlink has plans to bring trams back to the Palace.

Below: A military parade around the time of the Munich Agreement is watched by huge crowds as it makes its way past West Croydon, marooning an ex-LCC 'E1' on route 42, a London- bound 'Feltham' and a Country Area forward-entrance STL which has just set out on its way to Guildford.

Above: A 1929 Le Mans Bentley, identical to 'Beucephalus', which the author's teacher, Mr Critchlow, used to drive each morning and park outside Winterbourne Primary School, Norbury, in 1947.

Croydon when through-running began between Westminster and Purley. 'They [the 'E1s'] couldn't run on Croydon track as well as they did on our own. You could hear the wheels labouring; if they could have spoken they would have said: "I'm not satisfied with they way I'm running." ' I once rather alarmed my mother when she enquired where I had been on returning from a cycle ride, replying: 'The Westminster Bank ground.' I meant the local sports fields, but she clearly thought I had made a round-trip of 16 miles to take on the 400-odd trams which plied the Victoria Embankment from Westminster to Blackfriars each hour.

Sometimes funds extended to using public transport to get to school. This might have been by bus, either a 59A or a 115. Neither was to be sneered at, but they couldn't compete with the allure of a ride on a tram. Time considerations did not permit a choice of tram in the morning, so it might well have been a former Croydon Corporation 'E1' or an ex-LCC 'E3', but with time not being of the essence at 4pm I would invariably wait to return home in a 'Feltham'. Ah, the glorious 'Felthams'! It wasn't just we schoolboys who worshipped them. To quote Stan Collins again, 'We thought they were fine, just loved to get out and drive one of them. They were so modern compared with the Standards that we had. Drivers used to be disappointed if they looked up on the car numbers and saw they had a Standard. I remember one morning I went to work without my overcoat – I

thought I was bound to have a "Feltham" – but they gave me a Standard, and I froze until I was able to come home on relief and get my coat. They were a beautiful tram to drive. I can't praise them too much. After standing up all those years and then suddenly being able to sit down, it seemed impossible. And you had a cab heater. At first the passengers used to let the Standards go by just so they could ride a "Feltham"; they were that new. Conductors like them too, although they carried more people.'

I was twice blessed, for not only I did I live one road away from a tram depot, but many of the trams which passed along the London Road and could be heard from my bedroom were 'Felthams', which were right up there with such other icons of transport as Brenda Averty on her bike and the 1929 Bentley which my Year 5 teacher at Winterbourne, Mr Critchlow, owned and left parked outside all day, knowing that no harm would befall it. On the whole I was pretty lucky with my teachers; Mr Critchlow was of the first rank. He had, I think, come to us straight from the RAF; he had the requisite handlebar moustache and held us entranced with stories of being ferried out in a small boat to the *Queen Mary*, anchored in the Clyde, of climbing up a ladder ('like going up the side of a cliff') to board her, to be whisked across the Atlantic and taught to fly Lancaster bombers and various other aircraft, although rather to our disappointment but probably wisely he avoided dwelling on the horrors of war. He knew we lived in one of the most bombed suburbs of South London, and all of us had first-hand experience of air-raids.

No doubt it was Mr Critchlow's influence that persuaded me to buy a Dinky Toys *Queen Mary* (with wheels!) rather than a London STL bus from Wise's, the cycle and toy shop on the London Road (now 'A Taste of Jamaica'), when I found myself near the front of the queue which had formed following the discovery that the rumour that another consignment had arrived from Binns Road was actual fact. Production of Hornby trains, Meccano sets and Dinky toys had only just resumed after the war, and supplies were nowhere near sufficient to meet demand. I would have bought a tram, Dinky Toys No 27, price 3 old pennies, which in my 1939 catalogue looked very like an 'E3' or 'HR2' had one been available, but it never was, production not being resumed after the war. Mr Critchlow left us after a year to become the head of another Croydon primary school. I discovered 21 years later when a teacher myself that he was about to retire and went to wish him well.

Above: The low winter sun illuminates 'E3' No 1912 in London Road, Norbury, on 5 February 1950. It is hiding, on the opposite side of the road, Wises cycle and toy shop, where the author used to buy his Dinky Toys, although not the model tram (which was never produced in postwar days) which looked vaguely like an 'E1'. In the distance is another Embankment-bound 'E3'. The crossover in front of No 1912 was intended for rush-hour short workings but was little used. *J. H. Meredith/Online Transport Archive*

Left: North End, Croydon, August 1945. The war has just ended, and despite some 23,000 of its homes being damaged in the Blitz between September 1940 and May 1941 and despite its being the worst-hit town in Britain during the V1 attacks of 1944/5, Croydon looks in pretty good shape. Allders, the large department store on the right, had been badly bombed but is stoically hiding its scars as a former Croydon Corporation 'E1', rehabilitated by London Transport, passes. The picture was taken on colour film that the photographer, by now back home on leave, had bought in Canada whilst serving as a pilot with Transport Command. *Harold Bennett*

2

THE LCC

A postcard view, of Streatham High Road around the time of World War 1. 'E1' No 1082 is bound for Norbury, its route number displayed above the driver rather than on a stencil at the font of the upper deck as per later practice. It is moving onto a single-track section, later doubled. Built in 1908, No 1082 was destined to be withdrawn, still without windscreens, at Hampstead depot in February 1940. Two other 'E1s' are in the picture, the rest of the traffic being either man-powered or, in the case of the milk cart with its churns and the baker's van opposite, in the charge of horses.

I have Herr Hitler to thank for allowing me to become so intimate with the London tram (though I'm less grateful to him for twice bombing our house). Had there been no World War 2 the replacement of London's tram network by a trolleybus one, which was largely accomplished north of the river by 1940, would have continued remorselessly until trams were no more south of it either by 1944. As it was I was able to travel by tram both to primary and to secondary school for five years between 1946 and 1951.

Londoners got their first tram ride in 1861, the year my grandmother was born as it happens, initially between Marble Arch and Porchester Terrace (the trams, not grandmother), then, three weeks later, along Victoria Street and finally, in August of that year, away from the West End, from Westminster Bridge to Kennington. As Granny was born in a lodge in St James's Park she might well have ridden on these routes, but I never asked her. These first routes were, of course, horse-drawn. It is now over 100 years since the last horse tram disappeared from the streets of London, yet we can get back to those days in a couple of generations, for as a very small child our eldest son, William (now 42), met Great, Great Cousin Mabel, who could remember travelling by horse tram to meet her father, who worked for the Crown Agents in Downing Street.

The biggest player on the London tram scene would be the London County Council, but it was not the first to abolish the horse. This was the London United Tramways Co, which began constructing an electrified line – or 'light railway,' as a contemporary report described it – in March 1899 and on 4 April 1901 began carrying passengers, between Shepherd's Bush and Acton and Kew. Two years later the LCC inaugurated its first electric tram route, from Westminster to Tooting. Although a little slow off the mark the LCC would become the big cheese in the tram business, not just in London but outshining all other British operators, in terms both of

Above: A model – in the London Transport Museum, Covent Garden – of a horse tram plying between the Embankment and Tooting at Stockwell. Such archaic transport may seem to belong to the dim and distant past, but the author's three sons (the eldest is now 42) met Great, Great Cousin Mabel when they were small children, and she recalled travelling by horse tram to meet her father, who worked for the Crown Agents in Downing Street.

route miles (167) and of trams owned (more than 1,700). The trouble was that it got stuck in an Edwardian time-warp, and, although it continued to build tramcars until 1932, with the sole exception of the very last (the celebrated No 1) these were all of a design which dated back to the first decade of the 20th century, and yet many were still at work when the last was driven into the scrapyard at Penhall Road, Charlton, in the early hours of 6 July 1952. Yes, I know mechanically and electrically the 'E3s' and 'HR2s' of 1930/1 were an advance on what had gone before, but this was not very obvious to passengers,

Right: A postcard view of LUT No 87 – one of the company's original 'Z'-type cars of 1900, which inaugurated London's first electric tramway on 4 April 1901 – at the Shepherd's Bush terminus outside the 'Tupenny Tube' station in the early 1900s.

which was what counted. To quote Christopher Spencer, Tramway Manager of the Underground Group, writing in 1925 after a visit to America, on the rising public criticism of trams, 'This is not surprising, because there has been generally no noticeable alteration made as regards external appearance [since Edwardian times], and although the equipment has been vastly improved the only visible difference internally has been the use of white paint.' We'll return to this later.

The London County Council replaced, with greatly extended powers, the Metropolitan Board of Works. The 19th century had begun with the City of London much greater in importance, if not size – its boundaries having long been fixed within the square mile – than the adjoining City of Westminster and Borough of Southwark, but by the end of Queen Victoria's reign these latter had grown enormously, as had the many communities and one-time villages surrounding them, so that together they formed the greatest and largest city on earth, heart of the greatest empire the planet had ever seen. We late-1930s-vintage schoolboys knew this, of course, and took great pride in these boastful statistics, even if they were actually out of date or quite simply wrong.

It clearly made sense that there should be one overriding authority, and so the London County Council came into existence in 1889. It is perhaps a little surprising to learn that this was done on the joint initiative of the Conservatives and Liberal Unionists; who would have thought that Conservatives and Liberals would ever get together? The LCC ruled over 3 million subjects living in an area of 117

Above: LCC 'E3' No 1929, not yet fitted with windscreens, is boarded by a gentleman with a trilby hat, who may – or may not – be on his way for a relaxing afternoon amongst the sylvan delights of Highgate. The date is c1931. The track in the foreground looks to be in need of immediate attention. *B. J. Cross Collection/Online Transport Archive*

Right: An 'E1' on night service No 1 bound for Tooting c1946. *Photographer D. W. K. Jones, courtesy of the National Tramway Museum ©*

Right: There can be no doubting the popularity of the LCC trams in the first summer of peace after World War 1. Here a lady climbs aboard Forest Hill-bound 'A'-class bogie tram No 97 at the Embankment on 22 July 1919. Based (or 'shedded', to quote the LCC) at New Cross and Abbey Wood depots, the 100 members of the 'A' class – the LCC's very first bogie vehicles, dating from 1903 – survived until 1928-31.

Below: Everyone adopts a carefully composed, dignified posture for the camera, whether aboard or around Leyton Corporation four-wheeler No 57 in leafy Whipps Cross Road, offering a foretaste of the delights of Epping Forest awaiting at the end of the line. Pictured c1910, No 57 was one of 40 Milnes Voss-bodied cars of 1906. In 1921 joint working was established with the LCC, some of Leyton's cars being withdrawn in consequence; the remainder survived until the arrival of 50 'E3s' in the latter part of 1931. *B. J. Cross Collection/ Online Transport Archive*

Above left: A poster by Hobo Bros (G. S. Brien and F. Sherwin) commissioned by the LCC in 1929 and extolling the delights of Epping Forest, which was owned by the LCC.

Above right: Designed by K. James for the LCC in 1932, the last full year of the trams' separate existence, this poster is another that was somewhat economical with the truth; the open gate may indeed suggest the open countryside, but the wording beneath speaks of 'Suburban and Central London'.

square miles. The next tier down was occupied by 28 Metropolitan Boroughs. The common perception of the LCC (it was certainly mine) is that it comprised a bunch of died-in-the-wool revolutionary socialists. Not so – at least, not with regard to the revolutionary socialists. Yet it was radical and committed to social reform. It was much concerned with improving living conditions of slum-dwellers, and it saw tramways as a method of providing cheap, efficient transport to get the working-class Londoner not merely to his or her place of employment but also out into the countryside at weekends, to such rural (or semi-rural) delights as Epping Forest, Streatham Common, Highgate Village and Hampstead Heath and to various

Thames-side venues. From 1889 until 1907 the LCC was controlled by the Progressives, who were really Liberals, then for the next 27 years by the Municipal Reform Group, who were basically the Conservatives. Not until 1934 – a year after responsibility for the trams passed to London Transport – did Labour gained control, which it would retain until the LCC was abolished in 1965, to be replaced by the enlarged Greater London Council.

One of the first acts of the LCC was to decide upon headquarters. As all Londoners know, north of the river is where it all happens, and therefore many plumped for the West End. The suggestion that it should be across the water in Lambeth was greeted with horror by many – 'a very squalid neighbourhood', to quote one member – but, as another member pointed out, it 'would brighten a dull place'. And so it came to pass. In 1906 land was bought on the south bank of the Thames between Westminster and Hungerford bridges, and the 29-year-old Ralph Knott's design was chosen ahead of the other 100 entries; construction began, in no great hurry, in 1911, and was completed, again in no great hurry, in 1934. It can only be a coincidence that this was exactly the same length of time it had taken in the Victorian era to build the Houses of Parliament, on the opposite side of the river.

The post of Leader of the LCC, if not quite as elevated as that of Mayor of London today, was one of great importance. Between 1934 and 1965 it was held first by Herbert Morrison, then Lord Latham and finally Sir Isaac Hayward. All had considerable influence on transport in the capital and the suburbs, and all came from humble backgrounds, rising through the trade-union movement and the Labour party to be the top dog in London. Herbert Morrison, who became Deputy Prime Minister in the 1945-51 Labour Government, was, in his time, quite as famous as Ken Livingstone and Boris Johnson today. Born in Lambeth – it sometimes seemed as if he was tied to the borough by an umbilical cord – in 1888, he left school at 14 ('Secondary education was hardly thought of by parents of my class and time'), became an errand-boy, went to evening classes, got involved in the trade-union movement, helped found the London Labour Party and in 1929 was appointed Minister of Transport in Ramsay MacDonald's Government.

Lord Latham too came from humble origins, his first job being that of a clerk on the Great Eastern Railway in Norwich. Always involved in trade-union activities, he came to London in 1914, was elected President of the National Union of Clerks, and at the same time served in the trenches in France. He worked closely with Morrison, in 1934 being elected as Councillor for one of the seats in Hackney, where Morrison had been both Mayor and MP, and in 1940 succeeded him as Leader of the LCC. Latham believed that the LCC needed to expand, as London's suburbs had done, but although he had huge support amongst the electorate his ideas were not well received

Below: LCC 'E'-class car No 536 of 1906, fitted with a Hurst Nelson body and two Westinghouse Type 200 motors, on its way from Holborn to Hampstead c1934, passing King's Cross coach station and a substantial-looking limousine. It would be broken up at its home depot, Hampstead, upon being made redundant by trolleybuses in July 1938, route 3 being replaced by the 513, which worked from Hampstead around the Holborn Loop to Parliament Hill Fields, and the 613, which did the same journey in the opposite direction. Neither the tram route nor its replacements were normally what one could call money-spinners, and at one time London Transport questioned whether replacing the trams with motor buses might be a more economical solution; it was probably the fact that, on sunny weekends and bank holidays, the trams could hardly cope with customers eager to sample the delights of the open spaces of Hampstead Heath and its fair that tipped the balance in favour of retaining electric traction. The trolleybuses worked from Holloway depot, although Hampstead remained open for the storage of trams that might be needed to replace others damaged in the anticipated war and thus was home to redundant 'E1s' until 1945, when scrapping was briefly resumed.

Above: Quite the most famous location on the London tram network, pictured a few days before it all came to an end on the night of 5/6 July 1952. 'E3' No 1863 heads south over Westminster Bridge, a lone tram amongst five members of the replacing RT family. *Grenville Williams*

within the Labour Party, partly because some saw their own positions under threat and partly because of his determination to railroad through his own ideas rather than persuade by reasoned argument. This led to his resignation as Leader in July 1947, but later that summer it was announced that he was to become Chairman of London Transport – or, to be precise, the Executive which would replace the London Passenger Transport Board with effect from 1 January 1948. Although this change went largely unnoticed by the travelling public it was a highly significant one inasmuch as London Transport was now part of the nationalised British Transport Commission. The days when the great Lord Ashfield, its charismatic Chairman, and the even greater Frank Pick, its Chief Executive, were able make decisions without reference to a higher authority (and in so doing put it at the very forefront of urban undertakings worldwide) were gone.

Lord Latham it was who presided over the withdrawal of London's tram network, announcing in 1946 that the trams would be replaced not by trolleybuses but by motor buses and greeting the final car on 6 July 1952 with the immortal words 'Goodbye, old tram'.

Nor was there anything elevated about Sir Isaac James Hayward's beginnings. His working career began at the age of 12 down a Welsh coal mine. Trade-union activities brought him to London, where Morrison soon became aware of his abilities, and after election to the LCC in 1928 he was given the post of Chief Whip of the

Labour Group in 1932. At the same time his transport interests gained him the post of General Secretary of the National Union of Enginemen, Firemen, Mechanics & Electrical Workers. He served for 36 years on the LCC (a unique record), his unshakeable socialist ideals driving his commitment to the abolition of the Poor Law and its replacement by a proper system of welfare relief, to the building of homes with privacy for the elderly and to comprehensive education. Far better than Latham at patient negotiation and persuasion, he saw all this come to pass. An enthusiastic supporter of the arts, he was one of the driving forces behind the wonderful 1951 Festival of Britain, and the Hayward Gallery on the South Bank serves as a permanent memorial of his achievements. The one battle he lost was his opposition to the creation of the LCC's successor, the GLC.

One of the problems confronting anyone wishing to operate trams in the centre of London was the LCC's objection to overhead wires. Quite why the LCC should have been so uniquely adamant is not obvious. Other great cities in the UK – Glasgow, Edinburgh, Manchester, Liverpool, Leeds and Birmingham, to name but six – don't seem to have been duly bothered, nor were many overseas, one notable exception being New York. To be fair it was the City of Westminster and the City of London which were the chief objectors, and as they had control over their highways there was not much the LCC could have done other than try, unsuccessfully, to get them to relent. Indeed, they objected not only to overhead wires but to the very notion of trams. Here we come up against simple class prejudice. The tram, unlike the motor bus, was seen essentially as mass transport for the working class, and there was therefore no need for it to sully the hallowed thoroughfares of the City of London and the West End, where manual workers had little cause to be, unless needed for specific work. Of course this was the height of hypocrisy, but then I often wonder which would be the greatest loss to a community – its highly paid chief executive or its poorly paid street-sweepers. Nor was this just a British attitude. Frank Pick noted after a

visit across the Atlantic in 1920: 'Wherever a bus goes in America it seems always to charge twice the street car fare, and people pay it because it is fashionable to ride on a bus. It lifts you into a different social category.' Attitudes may have softened somewhat after the appalling sacrifices of the private soldier and the junior officer during World War 1, but by then London's tram network was all but complete and was already under threat from the motor bus, which was seen as (if not quite classless) suitable for conveying city clerks, West End shop assistants, college students and other members of the lower middle class.

The upshot of all this was twofold. Firstly all lines within the inner suburbs and which penetrated the fringes of the West End and the City had to be provided with conduit track, which was expensive to build and not easy to maintain, and secondly there would be no through routes across either the West End or the City, with one exception – the Kingsway Subway.

Below: One doesn't – at least this writer doesn't – associate trendy Chelsea with trams, but the short route 32 from Clapham Common just made it to a terminus on the north side of Chelsea Bridge. It was withdrawn in September 1937, a day or two after this picture of 'E1' No 1045 was taken, being replaced by a diversion of bus route 137. To the west, route 34 actually got as far as the famed King's Road, where it terminated, by way of Battersea Bridge. *Ian Allan Library*

3

PROGRESS

No 2225, built in 1911 as an MET 'H' type, a large bogie car of Brush design. The entire class was extensively overhauled in 1928/9, many (but not our example) being fitted with windscreens and ultimately becoming the last ex-MET cars in service, 'Felthams' excepted. No 2225 was withdrawn in November 1938 (the final members of the class going a few months later) and is seen here, shortly before withdrawal, at the Edmonton terminus of route 27. On the opposite side of the road, beyond the horse-drawn cart, is an almost-new Dennis Pax delivery van of the LMS railway.
A. W. V. Mace

London United Tramways was in two particular respects the most advanced and forward-looking operator of electric street passenger transport in the London area. One was its determination throughout the 1920s to push the design of the tramcar towards new frontiers, culminating in what became universally accepted as a vehicle superior to any other form of urban transport in the UK – the UCC car, or 'Feltham'. The other was not a tram but the first successful use of a fleet of trolleybuses in the London area, again fitted with UCC bodies, mounted on AEC chassis.

There are many instances of how the way things were done across the Atlantic influenced British tram systems. The beginning of this particular story dates back to 1921, when, after a visit to North America, LUT's General Manager, C. J. Spencer, had an MET four-wheel car of 1905 extensively rebuilt as a bogie single-decker for the LUT, No 341. MET and LUT were both part of the Metropolitan Group, and they worked closely together. No 341 was completely enclosed, which meant the driver was not exposed to the elements, as he was on practically all other London trams (and indeed buses) at that time. He also had a seat, but no conductor.

Above: 'Poppy', the 1929 experimental car built for MET by the LGOC at Chiswick. According to B. Connelly, writing in the *London Transport Magazine* in 1964 and whose memories of LUT went back to 1913, 'the MET were disappointed with the car', and it was duly transferred to LUT, becoming the latter's No 350. Being 7ft wide, it had two-plus-two seating on the lower as well as the upper deck. It is seen here in Chiswick High Road, on its way to Hounslow. Although it was in many respects a very modern car, the driver had no windscreen and would certainly have needed the stout overcoat he is wearing here.

Passengers entered via a sliding front door and received their tickets from an automatic machine; they left by a rear door. No 341 worked initially between Tolworth and Richmond Park Gates, and later between Brentford and Hanwell. It was a remarkably modern vehicle, much appreciated by the public although regarded with suspicion by union members, who, despite its improved comforts, perceived a one-man vehicle as a threat to their livelihood. Three more such conversions followed, Nos 342-4. Although not suitable for working heavily trafficked routes on which a double-decker, with a conductor who could collect fares whilst on the move, was considered essential, they pointed the way to a future which was as yet beyond the horizon but which would eventually come to pass as Croydon Tramlink.

Next we consider MET No 318, nicknamed 'Bluebell', although it was a good deal more substantial than the

spring woodland flower. Built at the company's Hendon works (later to become as Colindale trolleybus depot), it was placed in service in February 1927, more than a month earlier than bluebells normally appear, even in the mildest of springs, but by now both MET and LUT were well ahead of the game. Painted a brilliant pale blue and cream, No 318 was immensely impressive and put to shame all other trams then operating in London. Completely enclosed (although the driver's cab was initially unglazed), it seated 71 passengers, who entered at the rear and exited at the front; in modern parlance it was almost 'low floor', just one step being need to gain entry, and the saloon floors were covered in rubber. It was fitted with two Metropolitan-Vickers 101 motors, BTH controllers and Brush maximum-traction trucks, on roller bearings. Very large roller-blind indicators were provided which showed the destination, 'via' points and

Above: No 2289, a MET 'C1' type of 1907/8, at the Bruce Grove, Tottenham, terminus of route 39A (formerly MET route 18) in 1937. Waiting in the background is an ex LCC 'E1'. *A. D. Packer*

route number, just as comprehensive as that on any motor bus, although these still to a large extent employed boards. It also had air brakes, and these, sadly, played a part in the death of its driver, Maurice Kent, on 17 June 1927, when it failed to stop on Barnet Hill, hit a lorry and overturned. Hundreds turned out for the unfortunate driver's funeral. 'Bluebell' was duly repaired and

modified, being fitted with windscreens and a domed roof, which increased its modern appearance. Indeed, despite a plethora of windows it was now nothing short of magnificent. Repainted in standard MET red and cream, in black-and-white photographs it bears a distinct resemblance to Birmingham Corporation's newest tram, No 843 of 1930.

A little later in 1927 there appeared, under the auspices of MET but destined this time for LUT, another flower – 'Poppy', which, despite its coat of red paint, was highly inappropriate for what can only be described as a hefty, almost brutal-looking tram. This time MET turned to a somewhat unlikely source, the Chiswick works of the London General Omnibus Co (also part of the Metropolitan Group or Combine), and the result has sometimes been described as 'two NS buses, back to back'. It doesn't sound very appealing, but at this distance in time it is difficult to judge. However, there exists a rather handsome model; built by the late John Whitbread and now owned by John Prentice, it was on display at Acton Museum in March 2012. 'Poppy' certainly had presence and in some photographs looks really rather impressive, not least because of the domed roof. The cabs, which protruded from the body, lacked windscreens, but the passenger accommodation was completely enclosed. 'Poppy' was wider than contemporary LCC cars, with well-spaced and nicely upholstered two-plus-two seating on both decks. On the lower deck it had brackets, as on the NS, supporting the roof beams, cunningly placed to catch unwary passengers a whack if they stood up too quickly, but in most other respects its internal appointments were superior to those of just about all other trams and buses in London, 'Bluebell' excepted. Fitted with Brush maximum-traction trucks and Metropolitan-Vickers electrical equipment, it was originally numbered 319 but was soon transferred, in November, 1927, to LUT, which numbered it 350.

Left: 'Poppy', alias LUT No 350, at the Hounslow terminus of route 57 *c*1930.

Above: The late John Whitbread's model of 'Poppy'. Its bright-red livery is said to have given rise to its nickname, although, truth to tell, by the time of its build most LUT cars were already painted red. However, to quote Mr Connelly again, from his personal observation 'there were still some cars bearing the blue livery in Fulwell depot in 1933, after the take over by the London Passenger Transport Board'.

4

THE 'FELTHAMS'

An almost-new LUT 'Feltham' on trunk route 7 (for which the class was ideally suited), about to move from single to double track in Uxbridge c1931. In comparison with all the other vehicles (with the possible exception of the saloon at bottom left) the 'Feltham' looks like a visitor from the future. Immediately ahead of it is a GWR Thornycroft lorry. The GWR was a very good customer of Thornycroft's right up until nationalisation, and a vehicle similar to the one in the picture is preserved at Milestones, the excellent museum at Basingstoke, which was where Thornycroft had its factory. *B. J. Cross Collection/Online Transport Archive*

'Bluebell' and 'Poppy' both had short lives, unnecessarily so for such excellent vehicles, but London Transport, which took them over in 1933, had no time for one-off trams and soon withdrew them. However, in one sense they lived into the late 1950s for they greatly influenced the 'Felthams', the finest trams to enter general service in London. S. L. Poole, writing in the 1948 edition of the Ian Allan *ABC of London Transport*, described the philosophy behind the introduction of the 'Felthams' as being 'to combine in the tramcar all its own undoubted advantages, resulting from electric traction and the stability of a vehicle running on its own track, with the comfort and internal appointment of the most modern motorbus, so that as existing cars wore out they could be replaced with these modern vehicles. The cost proved to be very high, but as events turned out, the longer life of the tramcar has proved that the cost was lower than that of the motorbus or trolleybus, taken over a span of working life, seeing that the "Felthams", "E3" and "HR2" cars are still modern and serviceable vehicles, despite the fact that no extensive re-equipment has taken place.' (Not sure about the 'E3s' and 'HR2s' being modern, but we'll let that pass.)

The 'Felthams' took their name from the location of the factory. This was the property of the Union Construction Co, founded in 1901 by Charles Tyson Yerkes, one of the most charismatic and greatest rogues ever to grace the transport scene, an American who did much to create London's Tube network, at the same time managing to saddle it with huge debts. UCC, as it soon became known, remained dormant until 1925, when it was awarded the contract to modernise much of the Tube stock and, this having been completed successfully, to build 325 carriages. Then, at the end of 1928, work began on a revolutionary type of tram, and in April 1929 the first example, No 320, emerged. It is astonishing to think that this preceded the final batch of the LCC's 'E1s', the last in which came out in 1930, 23 years after the first. If the LCC was still looking back to Edwardian times LUT and MET were embracing the future. Yet there

is evidence that at least some in high positions within the LCC were prepared for a total rethink.

In a 1933 interview with A. D. Murdoch, Manager of Melbourne Tramways, Theodore Thomas, General Manager of the LCC tramways, commented that 'many of the large tramways had permitted routes to drift into a hopeless position by allowing their equipment, tracks, etc, to get into an acute state of disrepair, making a comparison with buses odious, and giving the buses a superior claim not justified by their merits'. Thomas had been in post only since 1930; had he been there earlier the story of the LCC tram in the 1920s and '30s might have been very different. To quote 'Kennington' in the *London County Council Tramways Handbook* (published by the Tramway & Light Railway Society in 1970), 'Under Mr Fell's management [from 1903 to 1924] modernisation and improvement were subjugated to the quality of maintenance'. But perhaps the most significant assertion is that 'Mr Thomas tells his engineering section that they should discontinue their 25 to 30 years' practice and build trams for a life of not more than 12 years, as obsolescence is a more important factor than depreciation'. If only.

Six months after No 320 a second prototype, No 330, was completed. It looked very similar, but its mechanical and electrical equipment was considerably different in that maximum-traction trucks (instead of No 320's equal-wheel ones) were fitted, the two motors meaning that the cost was reduced. This involved a redesign of the underframe. Both cars used air brakes. No 320, renumbered 2166, was withdrawn and broken up in

Right: Passengers board experimental MET 'Feltham' No 320 at Golders Green in 1930. *London Transport*

Left: The two experimental 'Felthams', Nos 320 and 330, stand proudly side by side shortly after entering service, probably in the summer of 1930. No 320 took up work on the Cricklewood–Whetstone route in May 1929, and its modernity took people's breath away, nothing remotely like it having been seen previously on the streets of London; No 330 entered service six months later, in November. Although, as can be seen, the two cars were very similar in appearance there were a number of differences, No 330 having reversed stairs, an altered door arrangement and revised interior fittings. No 320's trucks were not suitable for use in South London and, tragically and inexcusably, it was scrapped in 1937, when trolleybuses displaced it. No 330 was deemed suitable for operation south of the Thames and moved in May 1938 to Telford Avenue, where as LPTB No 2167 it worked until withdrawal in late 1949. *London Transport*

Below: No 2167 at the Elephant & Castle *c*1947. Alongside is a Fordson 10cwt van, and beyond that a Tilling STL, while in the distance is a large empty space, the result of wartime bombing raids. Just how regularly No 2167 actually worked from Telford Avenue is uncertain. As a small boy the author considered himself something of an expert on the 'Felthams', for in the fullness of time the entire fleet passed the top of Broughton Road in Thornton Heath, and the sudden appearance of No 2167, with its very different frontal aspect, came as a great surprise. That first sighting would have been after the war, and, whilst not as rare a beast as No 1, No 2167 was hardly an everyday feature of the tram scene on the London Road. *Ian Allan Library*

1936, and one would like to know why, for it seems a quite extraordinary thing to do with an eight-year-old vehicle of advanced design. I often used to see No 330 in postwar days, although because of certain non-standard features – one presumes these accounted for No 2166's early demise – it had been laid up during the war. Renumbered 2167, it worked the 16 and 18 routes postwar, and I managed to travel on it more than once.

The final prototype was No 331 (later London Transport No 2168), which was completed in June 1930. This had a centre entrance, four 35hp motors and air brakes and, most happily, is still with us, superbly restored to 1936 condition and in operation at the National Tramway Museum at Crich.

Two months after No 331 entered service it was announced that 100 production cars would be built, incorporating all that had been learned from the five prototypes. Delivery began in December 1930, 54 going to MET, 46 to LUT. Taken over by London Transport in 1933, they would outlive all its other trams other than No 1 and those preserved, the last being taken out of service on 7 November 1959, the final day of tram operation in Leeds, whither they had migrated a decade previously.

So what was it that made the 'Felthams' so special? Chiefly, as we have already seen, it was that, rather than developing an existing design, LUT and MET went back to the drawing board, starting from scratch, taking account of developments across the Atlantic and in mainland Europe and noting the rapid advances in motor-bus design, and thus came up with a quite revolutionary form of street transport that rendered all others following in its wake outdated. Inside the 'Feltham' was light, elegant and totally modern, better appointed than any contemporary bus. One only has to look at a photograph of a line-up of London trams to be instantly struck by the differences. The 'Feltham' is not only longer but lower, this latter on account of smaller wheels and a complete rethink of normal tramcar practice. It is also streamlined, with virtually none of the protrusions which were common on older cars (and

which today so delight visitors to Crich, who want to ride on something as old-fashioned as possible), the upper deck tapers inwards, it is fully enclosed, with four sets of doors, and it has a separate, enclosed driver's cab.

To quote Ken Blacker, in his book *The Felthams* (Dryhurst Publications, 1962), 'The aims of the designers had been threefold: to produce a modern vehicle with improved performance and with greater comfort for both passengers and crews … the result … was a vehicle which was truly remarkable for its time.'

The 'Felthams' were constructed along very different lines from conventional trams. Instead of the lower and upper decks being built separately, of wood, there was a metal, riveted framework, to which were attached lightweight steel panels. Aluminium had featured extensively in some of the prototypes, but this was considered too expensive for the production cars. Despite their great length the 'Felthams' seated fewer than did the 'E1s' (42 upstairs, 22 down), but this was deliberate, for there was a great deal of standing room in the vestibules,

Below: In the early 1930s Uxbridge still had something of the air of a Home Counties market town. Here LUT No 356, in its original livery, stands at the terminus of route 7 in April 1933. Many years later Mayor of London Ken Livingston advocated reintroducing trams on the Uxbridge–Shepherd's Bush corridor, but such plans were thwarted by short-term interests. *M. J. O'Connor*

Left: LUT No 354 working along the Uxbridge Road c1931. The LGOC S-type motor bus entering the picture on the left looks not merely antiquated but insubstantial in comparison.
London Transport

12mph, including stops. This speed was the highest that had been obtained on any urban tramway in this country.' A real thrill was to take a ride on a 'Feltham' to the Purley terminus of the 16/18, for, if one were lucky, once beyond the 'Swan & Sugar Loaf' and the 'Red Deer', where the traffic was much less dense, the driver might open up and we would simply fly along until, all too soon, the terminus was reached.

Stan Collins was one a number of drivers who couldn't resist the opportunity to let rip. 'I had the old booster notch on coming up Brighton Road and I was moving, when I saw a car in the nearside mirror, so I let that booster notch up and planted a bit of air to slow it down. When I pulled up at the compulsory stop at the Swan & Sugar Loaf the car pulled up alongside me – I thought it was the police but it wasn't – and a chap said: "Do

primarily for the use of passengers travelling short distances, which they were quite happy to do, for the 'Felthams' rode wonderfully smoothly. In this they anticipated the modern tram, both in the UK (Tramlink) and on the Continent. In tests it was found that loading and unloading was some 25% faster than with conventional trams. On account of their weight and their roller-bearings the 'Felthams' were also exceptionally free-running. To quote Ken Blacker again, 'Because of a combination of fast loading and unloading, together with quick acceleration and particularly efficient braking, the "Felthams" were able to maintain an average service speed of

Right: A former MET 'Feltham', LPTB No 2115, stands at the Tottenham Court Road terminus of route 21, ready to head back to North Finchley, in 1934. On the opposite track is ex-LCC 'E'-class No 708 working the 75 to Stamford Hill, whilst just visible is an ex-MET 'H'-class car. The contrast between the streamlined 'Feltham' and the upright, open-fronted 'E' and 'H' is most marked.
London Transport

Right: A gleaming No 2141, newly overhauled and transferred south of the Thames (although, of course, being on the Embankment it is actually north of the river), heads for Croydon and Purley c1938, pursued by 'E1' No 1804 bound for Wimbledon. Today trams have returned to both Croydon and Wimbledon but not yet to Purley. *A. W. V. Mace*

you know how fast you were going?" I told him "About thirty, I suppose." "Forty-eight miles-an-hour," he said. "I only paced you out of curiosity." Of course, trams had no speedometers, but then neither did prewar London buses and coaches. I once asked the driver of a 10T10 Green Line coach how he managed to keep within the speed limit, and he replied: 'I just keep pace with everyone else.'

There were a number of routes from which the 'Felthams' were banned, because of their length. As a little lad before I understood about depot allocations I assumed that was the reason they never ventured onto our local 42 route. But it was surprising where 'Felthams' might venture in an emergency. On a nightmare evening during the Blitz Stan Collins was working the 8, heading for Victoria, when bombs started falling. 'Rubble all over the tram tracks' blocked his way, 'another bomb fell in Higgs and Hill and the Sunnybank laundry caught fire'. The only way back to Telford Avenue was along roads from which 'Felthams' were banned, but despite threats from irate and doubtless rather nervous inspectors, with a mixture of bravado, bravery and skill he managed to avoid abandoned 'E1' and 'E3' trams and negotiated a bridge beside Battersea Dogs' Home, where he could 'hear the base of the trolleys scraping the bridge', before arriving at a sharp bend – 'I'm leaning out of the near-side cab window … the kerb's coming nearer and nearer … and as I came round the pilot gate just touched the kerb and then we were on the straight.' When eventually he made it back to Telford Avenue he was told by the inspector that no 'Feltham' had ever been around that district before and that he'd be up before the Superintendent, but when he was eventually summoned it was to be congratulated; 'He wanted to know how I had done it!'

Below: 'Feltham' No 2141 glides through Kennington on the circular Embankment–Tooting 22 route c1948. In the background is an early roofbox RT. *Ian Allan Library*

5

THE PICK INFLUENCE

Former MET 'H' type No 2264, working route 21 at North Finchley, looks in pristine condition, only the round-top lower-deck windows giving a clue to its Edwardian origins. On 6 March 1938 tram route 21 was replaced by the 621 trolleybus. No 2264 survived until January of the following year, by the end of which all the excellent 'H'-class cars would be no more.

There is no single opinion on what sort of man Frank Pick was. These are just a few: 'Intolerant, never listens – he knows all the answers'; 'One of the kindest men I have known'; 'No idea how to delegate'; 'The perfect listener – no one is more ready to admit you're right if you really are'; 'A great administrator, inspiring to work for'.

The basic facts of Pick's life and career are these. Born into a devout Congregationalist family in Spalding in 1878, he studied law at London University and as newly qualified solicitor joined the North Eastern Railway in 1902 as a management trainee. In 1904 he married Mabel Mary Caroline Woodhouse. When

Frank Pick. *London Transport*

in 1906 the NER's General Manager, George Gibb, was appointed Chairman of the Underground Group he took Pick with him, and by 1908 Pick had become the Group's publicity officer. Many years later, with typical modesty, he would recall: 'After many fumbling experiments I arrived at some notion of how poster advertising ought to be. Everyone seemed quite pleased and I got a reputation that really sprang out of nothing.' Amongst his 'fumbles' was the commissioning of Edward Johnston to design a typeface, of 'bold simplicity … belonging unmistakably to the 20th century.' The resulting Johnston Sans not only served London Transport throughout the century but still, in modified form, serves Transport for London and London Underground in the 21st. In 1918 Pick asked Johnson to redesign the roundel symbol which had been introduced on the Underground in 1907. The result was to become just about the most famous and instantly recognised transport logo ever devised, destined to copied and modified (yet never improved upon) worldwide. He also commissioned Harry Beck to produce the equally famous and much-copied diagrammatic map of the London Underground system.

Pick became the first Chairman of the Council for Art & Industry (later the Design Council) in 1932 and in the same year was awarded an honorary badge of merit by Josef Stalin for his advisory work on the Moscow Metro. Writing in 1942, a year after Pick's death, Nikolaus Pevsner would declare him to have been 'the greatest patron of the arts whom this century has so far produced in England and indeed the ideal patron of our age.' And this, remember, was a Lincolnshire solicitor without any formal art training.

Having been joint Managing Director of the Underground Group since 1928, Pick was appointed Chief Executive of the London Passenger Transport Board upon its formation in 1933. In a talk to the Board's chief officers he told them not to be afraid of 'a spice of vice [bet that made them sit up and take notice], a spark of irrationality, a fondness for inconsistency, a flash of genius'. He resigned in 1940 on a point of principle. In a letter to Trevor Hearing, who had been his secretary and assistant, he wrote: 'I got cross with the Board over Government control and its consequences. So I fairly had to leave.' Notwithstanding, Pick was appointed by Winston Churchill's wartime Coalition Government as Director-General of the Ministry of Information, which proved to be something of a poisoned chalice. In a letter to a London Transport colleague he opined: 'I fear my new venture may be hazardous. Political waters are full of wrecks and shoals.' And so it proved. Asked to approve the dropping over Germany of propaganda leaflets containing statements which, arguably, were not true, he refused. Churchill raged that it was a matter of the nation's survival, told Pick to get out of the room and shouted at his private secretary, John Colville: 'Never let that impeccable busman darken my door again!'

In the desperate, dark days of 1940 Pick's transparent honesty was not always appreciated. He refused both a knighthood and a peerage. Some people found Pick aloof. In the London Transport files there are numerous pictures of the Chairman, Lord Ashfield, joining in the fun of Christmas celebrations, handing over cups at athletics tournaments, bouncing bonny babies on his knee and generally being the life and soul of the party. There are fewer than half a dozen pictures of Pick, and all depict him in formal situations, looking rather solemn. Asked what working for Pick was like, Trevor Hearing said: 'He was interested in everything and everybody. Pick was always considerate to people junior to himself. But he was uncompromising in putting his views to those in senior positions … Ashfield and Pick understood that the well-being and survival of London Transport depended on the provision of the highest possible standards of service … Each had great respect for the other … But their experience and personalities were so different that their personal relationship was not close.'

So why did Pick take against the tram? His 1920 paper, read at a staff meeting of the Underground Group, supplies the answers. 'An omnibus route … gives some service that a tramway fails to give. A tramway represents an expensive mass of equipment. To put rails in a street to carry a light vehicle is a waste. The London County Council tramcar weighs, empty, 15 tons. A motor omnibus weighs, empty, just under 5 tons. The heavy vehicle affords more seats. A tram has 78, an omnibus 54, but seat for seat the omnibus is at an advantage in dead weight. More seats call for more passengers. A tramway requires a denser traffic than an omnibus route for successful operation. So a tramway must necessarily leave the working of the feeder roads to the main arteries, where traffic is lighter, to the omnibus routes. But who would want to get off an omnibus to get into a tramcar to continue the journey? So the omnibus runs through.' Another criticism of the tram was that it was often 20 years old, whereas 'The original omnibus has been scrapped for a new omnibus and almost before the new omnibus was upon the streets a still newer omnibus came into view.'

Pick had some interesting, surprising and profound things to say about competition. One would have thought he would have been all for it, but not so. He had sympathy for the trams. He quoted the situation in New Jersey, where, for instance, 'a crowd of small motor proprietors fastened themselves on to the street railways and robbed them of the margin of traffic which meant all the difference between profit and loss,' in Paris, where 'tramway and omnibus routes failed to respect each other's province and carried competition to a destructive pitch … and financial failure threatened to lead up to a traffic failure,' and Berlin, where, he noted, 'the State Railways failed to put up fares, being

Frank Pick and Lord Ashfield looking dignified and well wrapped up.
London Transport

content to meet the loss out of the imperial exchequer. The tramways had to meet this unfair competition … and after a while they were broken by the task and ceased working … who gained by this?'

None of this persuaded Pick that the tram had a future in London. Pick was adamant that London was a city ill adapted for the tram. The City of London in particular, which the tram barely penetrated, was a maze of narrow streets dating back to well before the Great Fire, and parts of the West End were little better.

He continued: 'The motor omnibus is the successor of the horse omnibus and the horse omnibus occupied those streets in London which are now traversed by electric tramways. The tramway is the usurper … One reason why London has remained a motor omnibus city is the narrowness of its main streets … A general requirement of all tramways [is] a clear space between the outer rail and the kerb of not less than 9 feet 6 inches. Yet this 9 feet barely allows for one line of traffic either side of the tramway, and is obviously inadequate to make proper provision for the other vehicular traffic.' Pick also noted that the tram network had to share well over two-thirds of its 348 miles in the streets and roads of London with the motor bus and implied that it would be better if the bus had a monopoly. In 1920, although motor-bus route mileage amounted to 577 whilst the figure for trams was, as we have seen, 348, the passenger numbers were very similar – 1,100 million annually for the trams, 1,035 million for buses; this could be explained by the fact that the tram routes were nearly all high-density, whereas many of the bus routes were not. Pick quoted his Chairman, Lord Ashfield, to back up his case for getting rid of the tram: 'Once a city passes a certain size [London was still, in 1920, the world's largest] the street railway solution of this traffic problem is seen not to have been the right one. The street railway is an intermediate solution good until a more highly specialised scheme of transport facilities is wanted.' So as early as 1920 the writing was on the wall for London's trams.

Pick was as far-sighted as anyone of his generation, but what hardly anyone could foresee 90 years ago was

Above: A fine old traffic jam at the Elephant & Castle shortly before World War 1, with a motley collection of London General B types and LCC four-wheelers and 'E' and 'E1' bogie cars. *London Transport*

Right: Another splendid traffic jam, this time *c*1925 at Aldgate, starring a wonderful collection of topless buses and a various corporation-owned East London trams, including some domed Ilford cars. The buses will eventually make their way through the City to the West End, but the trams will be turned back at the gates of the City. *London Transport*

Left: One of Leyton Corporation's 'E3s', No 202, challenges a brand-new Wolseley 12hp saloon for space outside Hale's department store c1936. *A. W. V. Mace*

Below: Barking Broadway c1935. Remarkably the antique-looking four-wheel No 39 about to set off on the local service to Chadwell Heath actually postdates the 'Felthams'; what chance of survival did the tram stand when a corporation such as Ilford was prepared to invest in something that would not have looked out of place 30 years earlier? There were eight of these cars, dating from 1932, which were sold in 1938 to Sunderland Corporation, which kept them at work until 1954. Behind are No 16 (another former Ilford Corporation car – this one dating from 1920), what looks like an 'E1' and, puting them all to shame, an almost-new STL cutting across in the distance. *A. W. V. Mace*

Above: The view north at Streatham Common c1925. A London General B type on route 159 (still seen hereabouts) is heading for the West End, and LCC 'E1' No 1142 is approaching on its way from the Embankment to Croydon (note that this was always given greater prominence than the ultimate destination) and Purley, as an assortment of rather fragile-looking motor vehicles, ladies with cloche hats, cyclists and others jostle for road space.

that the time would come when the motor car would have to be virtually banned from city and town centres. What was also not anticipated back in the early years of the 20th century – or, indeed, in the years immediately after World War 2, when proposals for wholesale rebuilding and vast new urban freeways involving the demolition of thousands of properties were being enthusiastically put forward – was that, however well intentioned, opposition to this 'Big Brother' attitude would grow to unstoppable proportions. We now recognise that certain routes will always carry heavy traffic – among them the southern approach to the heart of London from Croydon through Streatham and Brixton, the western from Uxbridge through Ealing and Acton, down the Edgware Road, the old Roman Watling Street, and from Upminster through Barking and Canning Town, to name but four – and that the high-capacity tram, be it a double-decker, like a 'Feltham', or a modern, multi-section single-decker given priority and reserved track wherever possible, is the ideal, environmentally acceptable means of coping with this.

So although ultimately I cannot agree with what my hero felt about the tram, we'll end this chapter with the final words of his paper of 1920, which rebut (if such a rebuttal were necessary) the notion that Pick was merely a cold, calculating administrator. 'I remember my last glimpse of America … I thought of my visit to the

Zoological Gardens … I was not to walk on the grass, or to feed the animals, or to eat roasted peanuts myself, or to carry a camera, much less to take a photograph, to smoke, to spit, to make a litter – I did not read all the rules. I hope I observed them. The spirit of liberty is good, but the application is merely moderate … However, the fog cleared and we weighed anchor and dropped down through the Narrows. Behind us we could see galaxies of lights, some high up as on a mountain side that reminded me of chalets in Switzerland, but I knew that the lights only came from upper floors in skyscrapers. The ferry boats, with their tiers of blazing saloons, passed across us. Piers and promenades gleamed from either shore. Strings of lights in lines betoked new townships. Strains as of a band reached us, and so through all this glory we slipped out to the unquiet, uneven sea, feeling for home.' Has there even been a more evocative description of leaving a great maritime city?

Above: A prewar picture of ex-Walthamstow 'E1' No 2055 at Camden Town on its way to Edmonton alongside STL420 bound for Chalk Farm, with ex-LCC 'E1' No 1268, without windscreen, on its way from Tottenham Court Road to Aldgate by way of many of the inner East London suburbs. *H. B. Priestley*

Left: As a 'Bluebird' LT disappears into the distance No 98, one of the East Ham Brush-built 'E1s' of 1927/8, stands at the Ilford terminus of route 63, ready to depart for Aldgate. Until 1933 operated jointly by the LCC and East and West Ham corporations, the 63 was one of the few East London routes which continued into the war, being replaced by trolleybus 663 as late as November 1939, at which point all the East Ham 'E1s' were transferred south of the river. *A. W. V. Mace*

Right: Not perhaps a wholly typical sight, this being the evening of the VE parade and celebrations in 1946, but the Embankment and Westminster Bridge could get pretty congested during any rush hour, morning or evening. The conductress of the 56 in her tailored slacks looks pretty relaxed, as if she is not expecting to go anywhere fast. Inching its way across the bridge is a wartime D-type Daimler working route 77. *London Transport*

Below: Westminster Bridge was certainly seldom without a number of trams heading across it, but this is really overdoing it, and presumably something fairly disastrous had brought all traffic to a halt behind the camera, in the vicinity of Waterloo station. However, that explanation won't really suffice, for clearly nothing is moving northwards. Although both lines of trams are stationary there would seem to be no motor traffic heading towards Westminster either, for southbound traffic, including at least one ST and a D, has spilled out on to the far side of the bridge beyond the northbound trams. Pedestrians are crossing the bridge on the east side, but we can see only one lady taking in the scene upriver. It's a puzzle. The war is over, and in those days there were no such things as security alerts. Of course, there were always traffic snarl-ups, but why should both directions be blocked? If we knew the date it might be possible to ferret out an explanation, but we don't. Various clues suggest the photograph was taken c1948/9, and, as no-one seems to be wearing an overcoat, it is presumably summertime, but that's about as far as we can get. *Photographer D. W. K. Jones, courtesy of the National Tramway Museum ©*

6

PENNYFARE

Pictured *c*1906 on its way to Waterloo Bridge via Old Kent Road, 'D'-class bogie car No 366 of 1904 has just passed Brush-bodied 'C'-class four-wheeler No 202, also of 1904. It had better not be in a hurry, however, for the horses dragging the cart which is holding up proceedings are clearly not Derby prospects.

Possibly the best source if you want to really know what life on the trams was like is London Transport's in-house magazine. Initially it had called itself *TOT* (Trains, Omnibuses and Trams) and was the house magazine of the Combine, but with the creation of London Transport it became *Pennyfare* and then, finally and rather unimaginatively, *London Transport Magazine*.

One very quickly becomes aware of how much horse-drawn traffic there was still on the streets of London throughout the tram era, and although numbers were declining year on year, encounters with horses were commonplace and sometimes needed quick thinking, as was the case in Canning Town on a July afternoon in 1933. For some reason a horse 'attached to a four-wheel van' bolted. Inspector John Tyler was standing by the conduit changeover near Becton Road. Seeing the runaway approaching, he 'without hesitation rushed towards it and seized the reins. After being dragged for about 50 yards he succeeded in bringing it to a standstill after it had collided with a stationary tramcar. Mr Tyler sustained a sprained right arm and narrowly escaped being crushed between the shafts and the tramcar.' The Commissioner of the Metropolitan Police brought Mr Tyler's action to the notice of the Carnegie Hero Trust Fund and also 'caused a letter of thanks' to be sent. Tyler was clearly quite something, for some six years earlier he 'stopped a runaway horse in Severn Sisters Road at great personal risk', whilst 'in June 1925 he left his tramcar and dived into the New River to rescue a woman and child'.

This is certainly not the only instance of a tram man tackling a runaway horse. Around the time London United Tramways was being absorbed by London Transport there is a report of Mr J. Ward, District Inspector, LUT, being congratulated by the directors of the Isleworth Brewery, on the courage he displayed in stopping two of their horses, which were attached to a dray, when they bolted outside the 'Coach & Horses' in London Road, Hounslow. 'Mr Ward, who showed great presence of mind, seized the bridle of the offside horse

Above: E1 No 1154 and inspector on the cover of the March 1934 *Pennyfare*.

and, although dragged along for about forty yards, managed to bring the animals to a standstill before any serious damage was done.'

Many of the senior men of the 1930s had started their careers in the days of horse-drawn trams. One, writing in July 1934, recalls his first day driving an electric tram with a conductor who was more used to horse power. He had stopped 'a bit too suddenly', and no-one complained except the conductor, who said: 'If you drove a mule like that tram he'd kick your brains out. Don't jerk on the reins, boy.' Another mule story is that of Mr Johnnie Woods. Three such animals were attached to a car which had left Waterloo bound for New Cross, but at the Elephant & Castle only two mules are now to be seen. Johnnie checks with the conductor, who confirms that there should be a third but cannot explain why one is missing, and it transpires that 'number three was under the car, completely out of sight. The lifeguard had "ridden" over the beast, which was a prisoner.' The story concludes with the punch line (which the editor of *Pennyfare* obviously considers highly amusing): 'You can pull a conductor's leg, but leave mules' legs alone.' All trams, whether horse-drawn or electric, had lifeguards which were there to scoop up any unfortunate pedestrian who might have fallen in front of the car and thereby prevent them from being run over by the wheels. Presumably the unfortunate mule was unhurt.

After '58 years unbroken service with the Tramways beginning in 1876' Mr J. Webb retired in November 1934. One of his earliest tasks had been to help 'break in American horses brought over for service with tramcars'. Later he became a horse-keeper, and inevitably the day came when one he was riding bolted; while being exercised on Clapton Common said animal dashed towards the pond, threw him in and cantered off to graze. 'Mr Webb *led* that horse back to the stables!' There was a category of drivers and conductors who, like stevedores (dockers), got paid only if they worked. To quote Mr Webb, 'No work – no pay.' He

Above: High Street, Putney, 1912. A cyclist turns to look at the camera, a two-horse cart plods southwards, a banner reminding the good citizens not to miss the Town Regatta hangs high above Wandsworth-bound Brush-built 'E1' No 1577, delivered earlier that year, and an LGOC B type bound for Willesden, whilst in the distance another tram and a B type have safely negotiated the crossing of the River Thames.

Right: The crew of a three-horse Wandsworth–Borough tram outside the 'Two Brewers' public house in Wandsworth c1900. *London Transport / Pamlin Prints*

also tells us that a conductor had to pay £5 deposit (more than a week's wages) as security. One who was refused its return threatened his manager with a revolver; fortunately 'he was overpowered in the nick of time'.

Another retiree in November 1934, at the age of 71, was Mr R. E. Grant, of New Cross depot. One night in horse-car days he was ticket-checking and 'came across two hefty navvies who pretended they had lost their tickets. Mr Grant knew [they] had not paid but the big fellows settled the argument by lifting him on to the top

deck and hanging him over the side!' In the same issue of *Pennyfare* we learn that a tram conductor worked out that during a day's duty he had 'rung the bell to start and stop 237 times … walked 1,884 steps, climbed to the upper deck 91 times, which means 728 stairs totaling 630 feet in height, cancelled 127 tickets, sold 565 and taken £5 12s 6d'.

By the mid-1930s the tram was on its way out, being rapidly replaced by the trolleybus, but it still had a big part to play, and from time to time *Pennyfare* ran articles dropping fairly heavy hints that just maybe London Transport would be well advised to think again. 'C. E. W. P.', for instance, writing in 1934, observes that 'special cars run for the benefit of patrons of football grounds, dog tracks and the like are not particularly remunerative; they serve, however, to illustrate the determination of the tramways to put service to the public first. It is fashionable, nowadays, to speak of tramways as being obsolete, and to charge them with being a main cause of traffic congestion. The up-to-date tramcar, however, with its smooth, quiet running, its comfortable seats and its excellent lighting, is unsurpassed for comfort and safety.' C. E. W. P. doubtless had the 'Felthams' very much in mind. He goes on: 'On a foggy night, the tram way is often the only way. The fact that trams are looked upon with disfavour by some road-users as being the cause of congestion is more than counterbalanced by their special usefulness in dealing with large masses of passengers during rush periods.' Pulling absolutely no punches, he concludes: 'London has reason to be proud of its tramways, and as a part of London Transport are likely to remain indispensable for many years to come.'

C. E. W. P. was clearly closely related to 'Cinderella', for in February 1934 this legendary character, believe it or not, takes up the case for the tram. 'It is true,' she writes, adjusting her glass slippers, 'that, like Cinderella, the tramways have performed an enormous amount of valuable work, but, unlike her, they have received no visit from a fairy godmother. Tramwaymen, however, are the very soul of patience, and they can be relied upon to give ungrudging service to the travelling public whilst awaiting the fulfilment of their dreams of pumpkins, gilded coaches or what not.' A financial case in favour of trams is then forcibly made by the estimation that, because of its obligation to maintain the roadway between and either side of the tracks the tramway authority, *i.e.* London Transport, saves the road authorities a quarter of a £million each year. It also pays rates of £31,000 per annum. 'Many thousands of postmen, newspapermen, busmen and other early workers have reason to bless the tramways for providing all-night and early-morning services, a means of transit when other forms of public transport are not operating … The tramcar also occupies the least street-space per passengers, and has the lowest operating costs per year.' Cinderella also reveals that London's trams carry 'about a quarter of the country's tramway traffic', that Greenwich Power Station, which supplied the Underground (and

still does today), 'consumes nearly 200,000 tons of British coal', that 'the permanent way contains 62,000 tons of British material' and that 'tickets swallow up 450 tons of pulp each year'. From the May 1934 issue we learn that some 3,000 tons of coal was consumed each week; 'obtained from the Northumberland district, being sea-borne to London in steamers carrying about 2,000 tons at a time', it was supplied by 'the equivalent of two ships and their crews throughout the whole year, while 550 miners are kept in regular employment, in addition to the workers on railways and docks.'

Another shy correspondent, prepared to reveal only the initials A. J. L., repeats a rather long-winded tale told by the conductor of a tram heading from Brixton Hill to the Embankment about a colleague who was suspended because 'He let a pole slip off the end of the wire.' The most interesting aspect of the saga is the point where A. J. L. muses as to the likely thoughts of the driver of the following tram, 'who had all the time been the silent but appreciative [we hope] recipient of our conductor's serial story'. He could, of course, only have been able to listen in by virtue of the fact that, like the majority of the 1,000-strong 'E1' class (withdrawal of which was about to begin), his car had no windscreen. It was at around this time that modernised versions of the 'E1s' began to emerge from Charlton Works. Despite featuring various improvements ('upper deck seats being of a new design giving greater length in the seats and more comfort in the backs … the ceilings painted in white enamel … the intensity of the new lighting [at] about a normal passenger's reading height being approximately nine foot-candles … linoleum on the floors giving a cleaner and more pleasing appearance than wooden slats … modernised ventilators') and being of generally smartened external appearance, the very first of the 'Rehabs', as they became known, were, remarkably, without windscreens.

Most tram drivers were able to make the transition to trolleybuses, although it took some getting used to and was not for all. *Pennyfare* conducted an interview with 'a 53-year-old driver' – and possibly at least reworded some of his comments. 'I have been driving all types of trams for the past twenty-eight years but after a week on the trolleybuses [consider] the latter are much to be preferred. At first I wanted to keep to the middle of the road, but that soon wore off. Yes, trolleybuses are a great improvement, and I appreciate the comfort and cleanliness of the driver's cabin.'

Sport and activities for children of tramwaymen

Above: A group of drivers and conductors about to set off on an outing from Bow tram depot in a canvas-roofed charabanc c1933.

feature prominently in the magazine. Just one example of the many reports of outings for children must suffice, being that submitted by Hendon depot in September 1933. Arriving at Sheerness at 11.30, 'the children were each given a present, oranges, apples, bananas and chocolates and 3d to spend. Tea was taken at the Sheerness Co-Operative Society's premises and was enjoyed by all. The weather was rather boisterous, but otherwise an enjoyable day was spent. Leaving at 6.15, Hendon was reached at 10pm.' One would have liked a little more detail regarding the 'boisterous weather'.

A remarkable sportsman was Conductor Walter Williams, who retired from Abbey Wood depot in April 1941. Before joining the trams he had worked at Woolwich Arsenal. He played 'first as an amateur, then as professional ... for the Woolwich Arsenal FC was formed of Arsenal workmen and played at the Manor Field, Plumstead'. A member of the 2nd Kent Artillery Volunteers, he served

Above: Retirement certificate presented to Frederick Thomas by the LPTB in 1940

in both the Boer War and World War 1. Losing his job at the Arsenal in 'a big axing process when the Boer War ended', he joined the trams at New Cross. The depot sports club won the Indoor Shield 13 years in succession. Walter also won the all-England one-mile cycle race in 1896, ran for Spartan Harriers (which were Southern England champions four times) and 'won a gold medal in the veterans' race at the LCC trams sports ... and spent most of his life as a member of committees, often as chairman also'.

A 1944 edition records the retirement of Mr W. Maggs, recalled as 'a chubby 18-year-old [who] straight from school goes in to bat for LCC Administrative Staff and scores nearly 100 – and the next time, and the next'. Captain of the team from 1926 to 1933 and also Vice-Captain of the LCC rugby team, he was a very different sort of Captain in World War 1, being twice mentioned in Dispatches; it is noted also that 'in *this* war his only son gained the M.C. for standing up to the bowling in France'.

In 1945 we are introduced to 'the oldest serving member of London Transport staff' – one Jimmy Affection, aged 82, who 'still does a full job of work every day as a fitter at Deptford Wharf [Permanent Way] Trams depot'. Although this would seem to be the record, it was not uncommon for the drivers and conductors of trams, trolleybuses and motor buses to work well into their 70s.

Inevitably it is men who dominate the pages of *Pennyfare*, but the August 1940 edition has the headline 'Sisters' 84 Years of Service at the Office Desk'. Lizzie and Marion Thomson retired 'within a fortnight of each other' and were interviewed 'in their comfortable home in South East London'. Lizzie began her career in 1893 in the office of the London Tramways Co (absorbed by the LCC in 1899) at Camberwell and retired as 'Superintendent of the 110 traffic clerks who deal with tram and trolleybus tickets at our Effra Road offices'. Marion was one of the clerks. 'It was a hard school and we worked long hours,' recalls Lizzie, for 'more often than not we worked on a Sunday and had a weekday off in lieu.' The interviewer adds that the Misses Thomson 'recall the changing dress and hair styles' and that 'Both think highly of the young women of today who, they say, are so independently efficient without loss of feminine charm.'

The light-hearted editorial tone is maintained throughout the World War 2 years, alongside lists of those killed and injured in the Services or during air-raids on London. In January 1945 a woman trolleybus passenger wrote to London Transport of the effect of a V1 'doodlebug' strike in Finsbury Park. The driver was W. C. Fowle, who had started his career on the trams. 'Although badly cut in the face, although blood obscured his vision, he continued to drive the bus until he got it into the kerb. There he assisted in getting out the bus seats for injured passengers to lie upon.' The lady goes on to wish Mr Fowle a complete recovery. Sadly he died some months later of his injuries. The Hon Secretary of the ex-MET Athletic, Social & Benevolent Fund, for which Mr Fowle was 'a keen worker', recorded that he was 'a good type, well principled, conscientious but retiring, *one of Wood Green's best*'.

Many stories of bravery by tram men emerge only after the war. Overhead lineman Thomas Stokes, a corporal in the Green Howards, managed to knock out three German tanks until 'Jerry machined us, he mortared and blew-up our gun … things were hot, but I got my section away'. He was promoted to Sergeant and was summoned to Buckingham Palace to receive the Military Medal before returning to work on the trams. On the same page there is a photograph of Sgt J. B. Shakespeare, 'who gave his life while rushing food to released prisoners of the Japs'.

After the war the trams were still living on borrowed time but were basically in sounder condition than a lot of the motor buses, many of which would be replaced before them. In the July 1948 issue of what has by now become the *London Transport Magazine* Joseph Schofield, Works Engineer at Charlton, perhaps not surprisingly mounts a robust defence of the tram. Commenting that there is 'little prospect of finding the eleven hundred odd buses which are needed to replace the trams,' he continues: 'And so the trams are doing a vital transport job; they are carrying well over five million Londoners every week. The men at Charlton and at the depots have set about injecting a new lease of life into the old tramcars. Already they are looking better – and they would run better if we could get more materials. The Permanent Way men … have to

Below left: An impressive-looking gent has charge of works car No 012 at Charlton Works, where it has just been overhauled, probably for the last time, *c*1938. A wheel-carrier, it had been placed in service by the LCC in 1909 and would not be withdrawn until the very end of trams in July 1952. *London Transport*

Below: Ex-Walthamstow 'E1' No 2055 seen on 2 July 1952 outside Charlton Works, where it was employed as a staff car. Judging by the upper-deck windows the weather must have been little short of scorching.

Above: 'E1' No 1597 of 1912 pictured c1938 inside an unidentified depot, although it could be Charlton, where it too has been employed on staff duties. On the left of the picture are a couple of 'E1s' not yet fitted with windscreens and to the right a substantial-looking Karrier breakdown lorry. Note the 20mph restriction, a feature familiar to all collectors of Dinky Toy lorries of this period. *W. J. Haynes*

patch, patch and patch again when new track, so desperately needed, is almost unobtainable. But in all weathers, often surrounded by swirling masses of traffic, they carry on contriving to keep things going and ensuring the safety of passengers.'

From an article entitled 'The Tram Doctors' (in the same, July 1948 edition) we learn just how much the tram system suffered yet still coped during the war. 'Every tram was shattered by blast at least once and many suffered many times, while the tracks were severed hundreds of times. Nevertheless, the Board's inviolable rule that only vehicles safe to operate should carry passengers held all through.'

But the end had to come. Before it did there were letters complaining that tram people were being largely ignored, so in response to this the October 1947 issue featured tram driver Edward Hicks on the cover.

Into 1952, the final year, and the trams – and, to a lesser extent, the buses replacing them – dominate the *London Transport Magazine*. There are interviews, pages and pages of pictures and even a poem by Sir Alan Herbert. Alfred Jago was chosen to drive the last tram. He began in 1910 as a conductor on the horse tram which ran between Woolwich and Charlton, 'punching tickets at night by the flickering light of an oil lamp'. Ironically the

standard LCC tram, the 'E1', was already in service in 1910; the final examples would disappear only in 1951, whilst slightly modernised versions would still be running on the last day. Compared with the RT-family buses which took their place they were as dinosaurs. Alfred Jago worked the Woolwich–Eltham route and 'came to know every cobble in the road'. He carried football crowds to watch Arsenal at Plumstead Bridge before the club moved to Highbury and during World War 1 might have had on board as many as 130 munitions workers on their way to or from Woolwich Arsenal. The introduction of glassed-in fronts proved a boon; 'I have come off duty sometimes in the winter with my overcoat one sheet of ice.' But there were pleasures too: 'Treasured among his tram memories are those early summer mornings on the Embankment and taking aboard the coster women and their baskets of flowers fresh from Covent Garden.'

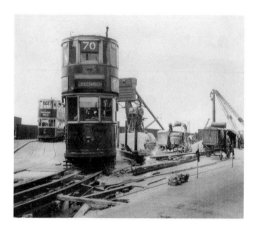

Left: The replacement of the bridge over Deptford Creek in the summer of 1949 resulted in this scene featuring 'E1' No 586 and another beyond. *Ian Allan Library*

Right: A tram driver (Edward Hicks) was the cover pin-up of the October 1947 London Transport Magazine.

Below: 'E3' No 1907 outside Holloway (or Highgate, as it later became) depot c1949. This was the last operational tram depot north of the river and was the second-largest – after New Cross – on the entire system. The conductor has put the pole onto the overhead, although the track is conduit. A horse-and-cart is minding its business on the other side of the road. Such sights were common enough on the streets of London into the 1950s; the Highway Code still demonstrated how drivers of horse-drawn vehicles should give indications when turning, and drivers of postwar RTs were also expected to use hand signals. *D. A. Thompson*

7

THE FLEET IN 1948

A nocturnal view of 'E1' No 1757 on the Embankment in prewar days, working route 14.
The lighting gives us the opportunity to have a good look inside and note that downstairs the
seats are nicely upholstered, as are those upstairs, unlike the wooden seats in the preserved 'E1'.
The boards along the side are replete with information *A. W. V. Mace*

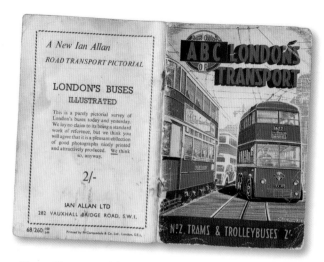

Above: The cover of the author's 1949 tram and trolleybus 'ABC', featuring an 'E3'-class tram and 'J3' trolleybus No 1039. The design was by A. N. Wolstenholme, who produced a number of attractive covers for Ian Allan publications at around this time.

We choose this date in particular because it was the year I bought my first 'ABC' of London trams and consequently was made aware that there was rather more to their categorisation than long and short, being enlightened not only by Ian Allan but also John Wadham and Clive Gillam, compatriots in Class Seven of Winterbourne Primary School who had being studying the subject for several years – something Clive is still pursuing, even if at a distance (New South Wales, to be precise), but we both lost touch with John at the age of 11. Clive continues to send me information and pictures relating to buses and trams in London, instantly, via the internet, the wonders of which still leave me speechless with amazement, especially when one thinks that such information when we were in class seven would have taken six weeks to arrive via a white-hulled P&O liner. London tram numbers ranged from 1 to 2167, but there significant huge gaps as a result of withdrawals from 1933 onwards, and the total on the LTE's books was 871. It was no coincidence that No 1 was very special – as, indeed, was No 2167. This latter was the surviving experimental 'Feltham' and regularly worked the 16 and 18 routes until, sadly, it was withdrawn and broken up at Purley depot in 1949. No 2166, another of the other prototypes, had long since been withdrawn (as had No 2168), which left No 2165, a standard 'Feltham', as the highest-numbered London tram until the final, extensive cull of the network began in 1950.

We young Thornton Heath-based enthusiasts regarded No 1 as the most exotic vehicle in the entire London fleet. Although it was not quite as advanced as the 'Felthams', these latter were everyday fare upon which we travelled regularly (and were certainly our favourites), whilst No 1 was almost ghost-like in its appearances, which were few and far between. It appeared only during the early-morning and late-afternoon peaks, on short-workings out of Telford Avenue on the 16 and 18, and then only when fancy seemed to take it – and never, as far as we were aware, south of the Pond. In fact it was the air brakes which were the problem, most Telford Avenue drivers being unfamiliar with them and therefore unwilling to take out No 1. It was elegant and shapely but not as long as the 'Felthams' and, as I became aware a few years later, not so very different from certain provincial trams of the early 1930s (in particular the Liverpool 'Robinson Bogie' and 'Marks Bogies' of 1933-6, which I got to know around the time they were being withdrawn and lined up on the scrap road at the Edge Lane depot.) Originally painted blue, it was always known as the Bluebird by tram men. Stan Collins described No 1 as 'a beauty, a pleasure to drive. I always called it my baby. It was

Below: Displaying a highly appropriate 'destination', No 1, the prototype of a fleet that never was (although both Liverpool and Leeds built cars that were influenced by it), swings off Blackfriars Bridge and onto the Embankment c1949.

Above: On one of its relatively rare outings beyond Norbury, No 1 glides along a damp London Road, opposite Thornton Heath Pond, with a full consignment of enthusiasts on their way to Purley. Once in a while it did reach the Pond on rush-hour workings, but on such occasions it almost invariably reversed there and scurried back to the safety of SW postal districts.

Below: The lower deck of No 1 as it is today, in preservation at Crich. It may look a little shabby, having received little attention in more than 60 years, but the quality of its beautifully designed fittings nevertheless demonstrates what a tragedy it was that the (almost) contemporary production 'E3s' and 'HR2s' should have perpetuated what were, in essence, slightly modified Edwardian standards.

really comfortable – the passengers loved it, and when I had it on Norbury extras they used to wait for it on the Embankment – and if you let it out it was really fast … On the last days of the trams at Telford I took the Bluebird out with a special party, and they said it was the finest ride they'd ever had on it.'

Apart from the 'Felthams' and the occasional appearance of No 1, on which I got to ride home from school just once, former Croydon Corporation 'E1s' and ex-LCC 'E3s' were our normal fare, these two being the only types which lived, like us, at Thornton Heath. The 'E1' was London's standard tram, and no fewer than 1,000 were built for the LCC alone, plus quite a lot more for the various municipal fleets that London Transport took over in 1933. The 'E1' when it first appeared in 1907 was a very fine vehicle. Although it was designed by the LCC, the bodies, trucks and electrical equipment came from various suppliers. Bogie cars always ran more smoothly than four-wheelers, and the LCC built examples of the former, the 'A' class, right from the start in 1903, although it also built four-wheelers, the 'B' class, which were designed for less-heavily trafficked routes. It is most fortunate that a 'B4', No 106, is still with us, at the National Tramway Museum at Crich, having survived as a snowbroom into the 1950s and then, eventually, meticulously restored to its 1903 condition. The 'Bs' were succeeded by the 'C'-class four-wheelers, and the 'As' by the 'D'-class bogie cars, and these in turn were replaced by the 'Es'. Tramcar technology moved on at a remarkable rate in Edwardian times and then, sadly, ground to a shuddering halt. There were 300 'Es', and they were succeeded by the 'E1s'. These were almost identical in appearance to the 'Es', and variations in both bodywork and mechanical design were minimal.

For its time the 'E1' was about as good an urban vehicle as you could get, with enclosed upper deck (although it would be nearly 40 years before all the poor old 'E1' motormen got windscreens), comfortable seats (although upstairs these were pretty minimal, the 'upholstery' being of wood) and much greater capacity than any contemporary buses. Indeed for four years after the introduction of the 'E1' a contemporary London General bus might well be horse-drawn, and, even after the last of these had gone to the great stable in the sky, the standard B-class motor bus was a primitive affair, with solid tyres – which ensured it did not ride as smoothly as the tram – and no covering on the upper deck (where the majority of its 34 seats were to be found), so that when it rained or snowed or a gale was blowing down the Thames from Southend passengers stoically accepted the possibility of pneumonia, frostbite and various other inconveniences. If you look closely at the expressions of upper-deck tram passengers in an 'E' or 'E1' overtaking a B-type bus at any time up to 1920 you can detect their smugness. Once into the 1920s this becomes less detectable, for buses had grown larger, suspensions had improved, pneumatic tyres had become the rule, and, glory be, that ultra-conservative body, the Metropolitan Police, had finally consented to covered upper decks.

I seldom travelled on a standard 'E1'. Once when I did, on the 20 – either because we were in a hurry and the parents were not prepared to wait for a 'Feltham' or because it was some sort of rest day (Feltham Festival?) when the 'Felthams' were allowed to have a lie-in and not emerge from Telford Avenue depot until the early afternoon – I was much amazed. Riding on the upper deck was the closest to travelling in a shed I that had ever experienced. In some respects it was unlike our shed at home, which was a rather gloomy affair, and as far as I could see there were no bicycles or sacks of coal lurking in distant corners, but otherwise the resemblance was remarkable. There was wood planking everywhere – floor, sides and ceiling were made of it, some of it varnished, some of it painted, all of it rather faded. Even the seats were made of wood. Whoever described such a vehicle as 'Pullmanised' should have been made to write out the Trades Descriptions Act in copperplate handwriting as many times as it took for him to admit the error of his ways.

The LCC's answer – and, indeed, that of the various municipalities (and, it has to be admitted, most British tram concerns) – was to continue with what had served

Below: Pursuing a 696 trolleybus bound for Dartford, 'E1' No 1316 pauses at Woolwich on its way to Abbey Wood c1949. Above the destination can be seen the three lights, originally of various colours, at one time used to indicate which route the car was working but long since painted over. One of the last trams to be fitted with windscreens, in April 1941, No 1316 would be withdrawn in November 1951.

Below: Looking down the front stairs, which passengers were not allowed to descend, at the driver of an 'E1' standing resolutely at his controller. *London Transport*

it well in the optimistic, Edwardian heyday of the tram. The LCC's priority was quality of maintenance, not innovation. It was an attitude which sowed the seeds of the tram's downfall; almost unbelievably, the LCC went on building 'E1s' until 1930, by which time the Leyland Titan and the AEC Regent double-deck buses were pouring out, fast and furious, from their respective Lancashire and Southall factories, and by the end of the decade they had driven the tram not only from much of London but from most of the United Kingdom.

There is much to be said for standardisation, and one can appreciate that it made sense to the treasurers of the various London boroughs when they reluctantly gave permission for their aldermen and councillors to replace their decrepit pre-1914 fleets with variations on the LCC 'E1'. West Ham, East Ham, Walthamstow and Croydon all invested in such cars in the late 1920s. The splendidly named Barrington Tatford, writing in Ian Allan's very first *ABC of London Transport*, in December 1944, noted that they were 'more modern than the E1 class proper,' although he might have added: 'but not by much'. Almost unbelievably, as late as 1932 – two years after the first 'Felthams' – Ilford was still investing in four-wheelers without windscreens. Leyton, on the other hand (and somewhat more adventurously), bought 50 of the 'E1s' successor, the 'E3', fitted from the start with windscreens, placing them in service in 1931.

To my infant and indeed later perception there was very little to distinguish an ex-Croydon Corporation 'E1' from an 'E3'. The 'E3' dated from 1931 and was preceded by the 'HR2' of 1930 – a type which had an identical body but, with four motors, was more powerful, being intended, as its title indicated, for hilly routes such as those serving Dog Kennel Hill, Dulwich and Highgate. The bodies were built chiefly of steel, but inside and out there was little to distinguish them from an improved 'E1' – a fatal mistake if the tram were to have an extended future in London. At least the second batch of 1931-vintage 'HR2s' had windscreens, but, incredibly, the 'E3s' did not. The cars

Above: The upper deck of No 1025 – hardly the last work in luxury, despite the LCC's having the cheek to call this 'Pullmanisation'. The seat bottoms may be upholstered, but the low seat backs certainly aren't.

Below: The lower-deck interior of the preserved 'E1', No 1025, with two-plus-one upholstered seating.

built with windscreens had metal-framed Alpax ones, which, aside from their primary purpose of protecting the motormen, enhanced the look of the tram, but those fitted later (and it was not until 1938 that all 'HR2s' and 'E3s' were so equipped) were wooden framed and although adequate, were rather less neat. In all there were 151 'E3s', including the Leyton 50, and 209 'HR2s'.

Above: 'HR2' No 144 doing brisk business at the top of Dog Kennel Hill, Dulwich, c1950. Note the wooden-framed windscreen, contrasting with the neater, metal-framed screen on the car approaching up the hill. *Photographer D. W. K. Jones, courtesy of the National Tramway Museum ©*

Left: A plethora of 58s, with Nos 115 and 134 leading, plus an 84 at the bottom end of the hill where the two tracks become four, c1932. Twenty blocks of slum-clearance flats were built alongside Dog Kennel Hill around the time that the 'HR2s' took over from the original LCC cars. Because, when new (as in this picture), they worked solely on the conduit system, none of the 'HR2s' was originally fitted with a trolley pole, and, whilst some later acquired one, others never did. *Photographer D. W. K. Jones, courtesy of the National Tramway Museum ©*

The slightly odd totals are explained by the fact that tram No 160 started out as an 'HR2' but soon donated its equal-wheel, four-motor trucks to No 1, receiving instead maximum-traction trucks as used on the 'E3s' and therefore became, quite logically, of that ilk. 'HR2s' Nos 101-59 were designed to work only on conduit routes and so spent their lives without trolley poles, as did No 160. One 'HR2', No 1858, of the variety which had trolley poles and a wooden-framed windscreen, has survived, and, expertly preserved, can be sampled at the East Anglia Museum of Transport, at Carlton Colville, near Lowestoft. If you are lucky enough to get the chance to do so you will probably reflect on how bright the interior is, for, despite my less-than-fulsome praise for a design which is basically of Edwardian origin, the big windows do give an excellent view.

As the 1930s progressed and the trolleybus took over from the tram, mainly north of the Thames, scrapping took place, not only of everything pre-dating the 'E1s' (as well as the LUT and MET cars) but also by 1938 of the 'E1s' themselves, so that by the time the last trolleybus conversion had been completed in 1940 more than half the 'E1s' – mostly but not entirely the oldest ones – had gone. There was thus a gap of just eight years between the entry into service of the last LCC 'E1s' and the first scheduled withdrawals. Most of the former municipal trams were also soon withdrawn by London Transport, but the most modern – all variations on the 'E1' except for Leyton's 'E3s' – were transferred south of the Thames for further service. For instance the 20 East Ham cars of 1927/8 went to Abbey Wood, and, rather remarkably, all but one survived until the very end. West Ham similarly had 31 'E1s', dating from 1925-31 (Nos 295-312 and 331-44), and these too were transferred to Abbey Wood, where most were also last-day survivors. No 295 was unique in that its body was built by West Ham Corporation in its own workshops. One much older West Ham car, No 102, a four-wheeler dating from 1910, was chosen for preservation; the sole surviving representative of the municipal fleets, it can today be seen at the London Transport Museum at Covent Garden. Walthamstow had 20 'E1s' of 1926-32 vintage, and these fled south to avoid the carnage. They were higher-powered than the standard 'E1', and as a consequence several worked out of Telford Avenue and Brixton Hill depots alongside the 'Felthams', with which they could keep pace. The Walthamstow 'E1s' received windscreens very early on in their careers, but of at least

Above: The upper deck of 'HR2' No 1858, now preserved at the East Anglia Transport Museum. The large windows and the glossy finish to the ceiling give a light and airy effect.

Above: Who are you and where are you going? A former Walthamstow Corporation 'E1', No 2054, on route 16 (we have to take the photographer's word for this) heads through the slush covering Westminster Bridge Road, with a GPO Morris Commercial van in the distance, on New Year's Day 1951. *J. H. Meredith/Online Transport Archive*

two different types. Actually there were all sorts of subtle variations on the windscreen theme; some of the Walthamstow cars sported a style which gave them a rather tubby and, I thought, quite impressive aspect – or at least as a small child I did, imagining that this in some way qualified them to compete on almost equal terms with the 'Felthams'.

Route-number indicators also varied. The early LCC standard was a stencil which at night was illuminated by the car's interior lights, but later a much larger, more impressive metal one was employed. This was commonplace in Croydon, featuring on the majority of ex-Corporation and ex-Walthamstow 'E1s' and the 'E3s'

Below: A scene outside Catford bus garage *c*1948. Centre-stage is tram No 574, one of the final batch of 1930-vintage 'E1s' with English Electric bodies, and trucks and electrical equipment from the Kingsway Subway single-deck cars, the easiest identifiable distinguishing feature being the large stencil numbers, as applied to the later municipal 'E1s' and the 'E3s' and 'HR2s'. Playing a subsidiary role are a GPO Telephones Morris 8 van and two early roofbox RTs still in their original livery with cream upper-deck window frames – on the left Saunders-bodied RT1387, on the right Weymann-bodied RT486. Both were based at Catford, the garage being just out of sight to the left of the picture. Vehicles aside, little here has changed in 66 years. *A. W. V. Mace*

– but not, of course, on the 'Felthams' and the rehabilitated ex-Corporation 'E1s', which had roller blinds. The East Ham and West Ham cars had another, much smaller indicator, although they also had a roller blind for the route number.

Having touched on the matter of rehabilitated trams we should perhaps elaborate on the subject. In the mid-1930s London Transport decided that something ought to be done to improve the image of the time-expired, antediluvian 'E1' and announced that up to 1,000 of them, mostly working south of the river, would be modernised. In the event significantly fewer (a mere 162) were treated – largely, it would appear, because Pick felt that as little money as possible should be spent on the tram fleet. The most noticeable internal differences were much-improved upholstered seating on both decks, bus-type press-button bells (instead of the plunge-type originals which, unless struck fair and square, were adept at inflicting an impressive bruise) and white-painted, plywood ceilings. Externally there were roller-blind route and number indicators and flush panelling on both decks. What was lacking, initially, was windscreens – an omission difficult to comprehend when one considers that by this date (1935) the standard trolleybus, with all its refinements, was in production. Another surprise was that many of the

cars chosen for rehabilitation were already the best part of 30 years old, rather than more moderns ones, although four modern 'HR2s' and four of the 'E1s' bought by Croydon Corporation in 1926/7 were also modernised; no reason seems to have been uncovered for this curious anomaly. I've often wondered why the Croydon rehabs made so little impression upon me, for I often travelled on them – one, No 396, was destroyed in the Blitz, but the other three survived until the end of trams in Croydon, the first time around – and can only conclude it as because they were little different internally from the other ex-Croydon cars and the LCC 'E3s'. Certainly on the rare occasions when I found myself unable to board a 'Feltham' at Brixton and had to make do with an original 'E1' its interior came as quite a culture shock. Although Oakley and Holland, in their magisterial work *London Transport Tramways 1933-52* (London Tramways History Group, 1998), comment that after postwar overhaul the rehabilitated cars proved 'sturdy' and 'robust', one wonders if this was entirely accurate, for they also note that 35 were withdrawn at the very first stage of tramway abandonment, before many of the unmodernised 'E1s', and none survived Stage 6, in January 1952.

Apart from No 1 there were a handful of cars which resembled it in certain respects and were the only ones, besides it and the 'Felthams', that actually looked

Above: The lower deck of a rehabilitated 'E1' in service. This is No 1103 of 1908 vintage – a year newer than the preserved No 1025 – with a Hurst Nelson rather than an in-house LCC body. The seats are a good deal more luxurious, and the tongue-and-groove panelled roof has been replaced with plain sheeting.

Below: At least nine trams are visible in this photograph, taken outside New Cross depot on a grey, wintry-looking day c1950. Nearest the camera is 'E1' No 1602, a Brush-bodied car of 1912, beyond which are an 'E3', a rehabilitated 'E1' and more 'E1s' and 'E3s'. In its later years New Cross had a reputation of being a somewhat awkward depot to deal with, personality-wise, and its trams were not the best maintained in London. *A. W. V. Mace*

modern. The three members of the 'ME3' class had a most curious reincarnation, for they started out in 1910 as Class M, being basically four-wheel versions of the 'E1'. They might have been better suited working in Blackpool, for by all accounts their ride was at times reminiscent of a rollercoaster. Eventually, to quote S. L. Poole's 1949 'ABC', 'their bodies were cut in two halves and a length spliced in the centre, making the bodies the same length as the standard "E1" class … No 1441 was destroyed by fire in 1943, 1370, which was rebuilt from "M" class No 1446, on reconstruction had an entirely new top deck and is now classified "E1r", while 1444 was fitted with the present wood constructed top cover after being damaged in a depot accident.' These, along with car No 2, were far from 'standard E1s', for they had similar top decks to No 1's, with domed roofs, which improved their looks immeasurably, and roller-blind route and number indicators. No 2 could claim to be the only tram actually built by London Transport, being a complete rebuild of the original No 1370, which was badly damaged in June 1933. I used to see No 2 and the 'new' No 1370 working along the Embankment, and their greatly enhanced appearance relative to the 'E1s' and 'E3s' never failed to impress.

Above: A much-modernised (as opposed to merely rehabilitated) 'E1' was 'No 1260, which was rebuilt, following collision damage, at Charlton Works in June 1935. *D. A. Thompson*

Below: No 2, a most handsome car, outside the Gaumont, Lewisham, on its way to Victoria. Approaching in the distance is an 'RT3' in original livery, whilst on the left is a 1939 Series E Morris 8. No 2 was rebuilt in February 1935 using the frame and trucks of the original No 1370 and was given a domed aluminum-alloy roof, tapering upper-deck window frames and recessed roller-blinds indicators, which resulted in a vehicle that looked vastly more modern than any of the numerous 'E1' variations, the 'E3s' or the 'HR2s'. *A. W. V. Mace*

Above: Very similar in appearance to No 2 was No 1370, a drastic 1933 reconstruction of damaged four-wheel M-class car No 1446. The first of the small group of much modernised trams produced at the very end of the LCC era, it is seen *c*1948 passing the Catford garage of the well-known South London coach firm of Timpson's. *A. W. V. Mace*

Right: A line of trams – an 'HR2' on route 56, followed by a rehabilitated car (either an 'HR2' or an 'E1') and three other cars – is held up whilst emergency work is completed on the track, the crowd of interested spectators including some of the tram crews. Watching people at work was ever a compelling pastime. *Ian Allan Library*

Right: A number of trams received thorough overhauls at Charlton Works in the late 1940s and as a consequence looked good for many years more. One such was 'HR2' No 149, seen here on the Embankment *c*1949. *Ian Allan Library*

Below: 'E1' No 1784 of 1922 at Camberwell *c*1948, with an 'HR2' ahead of it and an STL on route 68 leading the way. No 1784 retains its original colour-light indicators, albeit now painted over. *Ian Allan Library*

Bottom: A line of Victoria-bound trams stands on Vauxhall Bridge in 1947. Bringing up the rear is ex-Walthamstow 'E1' No 2053 of Telford Avenue depot, with two other 'E1s' immediately ahead and the very different profile of a 'Feltham' in the lead.

Right: Two 'E3s', No 1988 leading, at the North London Manor House terminus of route 33 c1948. In postwar years trams were interlopers in this part of London, which was very much trolleybus territory; routes 31, 33 and 35 survived only because they passed through the Kingsway Subway. *A. W. V. Mace*

Left: A neat-and-tidy-looking 'HR2' No 133 passing an estate of prefabs erected on a bombsite in Peckham. Judging by the women's attire it is summertime, possibly 1949.

Right: Pictured c1950, an 'E1' has just set off from its terminus outside Wimbledon Town Hall and is bound for Tooting, Clapham, Stockwell and the Embankment on route 4. Some of the oldest cars in the fleet worked routes 2 and 4 from Clapham depot, and this one has strengthening strapping on the lower deck.

Left: Grove Park on 27 August 1949. A pair of rehabilitated 'E1s', No 1310 leading, is just setting off, although the driver has not yet changed the indicator, whilst No 1491 sits behind. *J. H. Meredith/Online Transport Archive*

Middle: Victoria, 2 September 1948. 'Feltham' No 2133 is setting off down Vauxhall Bridge Road on the Tooting circular route 8 as an 'HR2' waits to move up into the terminal stub. An STL demonstrates what the trams could never do, which is continue on through the heart of the West End, across Buckingham Palace Road, around Hyde Park Corner and on past Marble Arch. *B. T. Cooke/B. J. Cross Collection*

Below: Newly overhauled 'Feltham' No 2143 at Stockwell on 14 October 1950, with a wartime D-class Daimler from Merton garage alongside. Just managing to get into the picture are two commercial vehicles which were a familiar sight at this time; on the far right is an *Evening News* Commer van, whilst tucked behind the 'Feltham' is a United Dairies Scammell. *J. H. Meredith/Online Transport Archive*

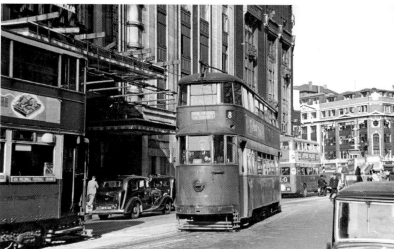

8

A JOURNEY THROUGH SUBURBIA

'E3' No 1930 heads south past Streatham Common on 4 March 1951, pursued
by a very interesting-looking vehicle from across the Atlantic.
J. H. Meredith/Online Transport Archive

The London tram's natural habitat was suburbia. Only grudgingly was it permitted into the West End and the City, and then only on the fringes. Although the most eagerly anticipated tram journeys I made were those to the heart of London – to the Embankment by the 16 or 18, to Victoria by the 8 or 20 and to the 'City and Southwark', as the indicator on route 10 proclaimed – I would guess that something like 95% of my tram travels were confined to the suburbs. As I grew older and, as I unwisely thought, wiser, 'suburban' became almost a derogatory term for dull, mean, bourgeois uniformity, and by the time I was in my 20s I agreed with my fellow art students that the only 'real' place for a creative soul to flourish was in a city, preferably London, Paris, New York, or San Francisco – or, for a few years, Liverpool. Yet I knew that my tram journeys of 10 or so years earlier through South London had captivated me, not merely on account of the network of lines, the depots, the conduit change-points and the tramcars themselves but of the places through which we passed, of the varying styles of buildings ranging from Victorian tenements to art-deco flats, of railway bridges high and low (I'm thinking particularly of Brixton), of the bright-red motorcycle shops of Pride & Clarks lining much of the Stockwell Road, of the towering Town Hall at the bottom of Brixton Hill which, confusingly, was referred to as Lambeth, of the nursery near Kennington where the small children always seemed to be outside playing and were gradually becoming more multi-ethnic, of the odd patches of green surrounding churches of grey (possibly once white) and brown brick, of the many gaps where bombs had fallen, of prefabs on Streatham Common, of a glimpse of the Oval cricket ground, where in August 1948 I would see Bradman play his last test match (and where Neville Cardus would arrive by tram), of being lucky not to have my sandwiches sat upon as the tram – almost certainly a 40-year-old 'E1' – bounced and rattled on the uneven track, of the sight of two seemingly endless rows of trams stretching almost to the Houses of Parliament- and St Paul's-dominated horizon as I

Below left: An LCC poster for Streatham Common and the Rookery, the latter a landscaped, wooded garden area with streams and winding paths – a favourite destination of the author's, where he could pretend to be driving a 'Feltham' whilst making appropriate hissing noises. It seems the LCC's publicity department too was prone to flights of fancy, for only the 16 and 18 actually ran past Streatham Common, the other routes getting no closer than St Leonard's Church, just north of the changeover point beside Streatham station and the best part of a mile distant. And if the 20 to Victoria was included, why not its companion Tooting-circular route 8 also? *London Transport*

Below right: An LCC poster dating from 1926 and designed by Agnes D. Gower. We do not know much about Ms Gower, although she certainly had an excellent sense of design and was probably a student at the LCC's Central School of Art & Design, which received many commissions around this time. Purley was the furthest south reached by London's tram network and before World War 1 was on the edge of the country, although by the mid-1920s ribbon development was spreading along the A23 Brighton Road towards Coulsdon, whilst up on the downs the exclusive Foxley estate was being built, including an avenue dedicated to those who had died in the fighting at Verdun. *London Transport*

Above: Former Leyton 'E3' No 201 heads along a damp North End, Croydon's principal shopping thoroughfare, on 17 March 1951, less than three weeks before the end of Croydon's first generation of trams. The wet weather certainly hasn't dampened the shoppers' enthusiasm to be out and about, while headscarves are very much in fashion. In the distance can be seen at least three RTs, replacements for the ancient petrol-engined STs and early STLs with which Croydon garage (TC) was saddled until 1949/50. Soon many more RTs would appear – on the 109, which would replace the 16 and 18, and the 190, which would replace local route 42. *Pamlin Prints/Online Transport Archive*

sat at the front of the upper deck in command of a number 16 or 18 as it attained the brow of the hill by Telford Avenue depot or, in a very different suburban milieu, of speeding on a 'Feltham' past the leafy, semi-detached villas on the long, final straight run beyond the 'Red Deer' to Purley, the southern extremity of London's tram network.

There was a great variety of cinemas and theatres between Croydon and Kennington. In the tram era Croydon had at least four that I knew. The Grand was just a hundred yards or so from where route 42 terminated – in the middle of the busy main road – and reversed. Dating from 1896, it really was rather grand although quite small. Our family used to watch repertory and musical plays there, and my father once inadvertently got involved in audience participation when he blew his nose loudly (which I always found desperately embarrassing) as a tenor was performing and who broke off to look up and say 'Thankyou, sir.' When it was threatened with closure in the late 1950s we art students got involved in trying to save it, helping to collect 10,000 signatures and having a whale of a time in being allowed backstage. Unfortunately the manager, whom we thought a wonderful, charismatic chap, absconded with the takings one night, never to be seen again, and that was the end of the poor old Grand.

A few yards up the road was the Davis Cinema. Opened in 1928, it could seat no fewer than 3,725,

making it, briefly, the largest in the United Kingdom. As a trainee reporter on the *Croydon Advertiser* in the 1950s I used to get free tickets, and I have seen it full to capacity. It lost a few of those 3,725 seats when *Rock around the Clock* was shown, and the audience got up to dance and had to remove some to create more space; I was not there that night. It continued to put on stage shows until the end, which came in 1959. Ella Fitzgerald, Buddy Holly and the Bolshoi Ballet all appeared, although, sadly, not on the same night.

The Empire was also on the 16/18/42 tram routes, in North End. Dating from way back, 1800 to be precise, it had been much rebuilt by the time of my only visit, by tram, in 1949 to see Jimmy Hanley, the sensation of the minute on account of starring in the film *The Blue Lamp* with Jack Warner. The latter, despite playing a character who dies in the film, was miraculously revived to star for donkeys years on TV as *Dixon of Dock Green*. On the bill was a comedian who seemed positively to dislike his audience and set about being as insulting to them as possible; I felt most uncomfortable. If he ever made it onto the radio or TV he escaped my notice, thank goodness.

We now come to the only theatre where 'yours truly' played a starring role. If you think we are straying further and further from the subject in hand, *i.e.* London trams, not so, for this is the only theatre which they still pass directly, or would if the building were still there. The Civic Hall was in Crown Hill, down which Tramlink descends, just below the Tudor Alms Houses (routes 16, 18 and 42 used also to pass the Alms Houses), and in it all sorts of performances were given, mostly by amateurs. Hence my appearance as the villain in Thomas Dekker's *The Witch of Edmonton*, a 17th-century play about a resident of that North London borough who sold her soul to the Devil, having given up hope on a damp, miserable February afternoon that the long-awaited No 49 tram would ever appear. (Actually I made up that last bit; the 49 was known for its punctuality.) One of Croydon Art School's specialities was theatre design, and every year a play would be staged in which the theatre department could display its talents. Unfortunately many of the performers were rather less talented; we were there, after all, to become world famous painters, industrial designers, potters or whatever, not actors, but were enticed, bullied or blackmailed into appearing on stage. The theatre critic of the *Croydon Advertiser*, perhaps out of pity for a former colleague, did not mention me by name but was rather harsh on most of our performances, accusing the hero, Tony, of 'cringing in his costume' – so of course for years afterwards we, his dear friends, would call out from time to time across the life drawing studio, 'Stop cringing, Tony!' The following year proper actors from one of the London drama schools were employed. Actually art school and the stage were pretty well entwined in those days. Ray Davies, of The Kinks fame (probably the best lyric-writer of his generation, save Lennon and McCartney – 'Waterloo Sunset' and other songs include many references to

The ornate auditorium of Streatham Hill Theatre, March 2012.

London's trains and buses, being just a bit late for trams), was among the students at Croydon Art School

Brixton was a great place for the theatre- and film-goer. The first one our 16 or 18 tram came to was the Palladium (not *the* Palladium) on Brixton Hill, next door to the Town Hall. Originally a theatre, it had become a cinema in 1929 and is still there, as a nightclub, but with a radically altered façade. One of the finest cinemas of the 1920s and '30s anywhere was the Odeon, which had opened in 1929 as the Astoria. Built in the Italian Renaissance style, it also is still there, listed and substantially restored. Less fortunate was the Empress, which never became a cinema and remained a theatre post 1945. In that year Cavanagh O'Connor, an Irish tenor who styled himself 'The Strolling Vagabond', was on the bill. I used to hear him regularly on *Variety Bandbox* on the Light Programme and was always impatient for him to get to the end of one of his sentimental ditties about his elderly beshawled mother slaving over an open fire in her mud-walled cottage in Connemara – I believe he had actually provided her with a rather nice semi-detached villa in Pinner – so that I could fall about at the quips of Frankie Howerd or Arthur English.

Then there was Albert Modley. He was one of the best of the dozens of top-rate comedians Lancashire has bred in order to make the world a jollier place. One of the stalwarts of *Variety Bandbox*, Albert, besides telling jokes, used to play the drums and brought his act to a climax by turning his drum set into the controls of a tram, although one needed television, which we could view only by invitation from Mrs Moore next door, who was almost the first in our road to buy a set (a TV, not a drum kit – not Mrs Moore's style at all), to appreciate the full effect of this. If he'd been on the scene a bit later Albert would have fitted perfectly into the cast of *Last of the Summer Wine*. His catchphrase was 'Eeeh, isn't it grand when you're daft?' which actually was the last thing he was. Albert's career began on the Midland Railway in the parcels office at Ilkley, where he used to entertain passengers who had missed their train; after seven years gave up the railways for a full-time career in clubs, then music hall. When driving his tram – its destination was always 'duplicate',

Top right: Streatham High Road, 15 June 1949. This was one of the very few stretches of road in the London suburbs that was wide enough to allow a partial separation of tram tracks from other traffic. Passengers are boarding and alighting from 'Feltham' No 2126 by way of a raised platform as an STL passes by on its way to Clapham Common, where it will meet several more tram routes. Honesty compels the author to admit that he once got travel-sick on a 'Feltham' (of all vehicles!) and had to make a hasty exit from it here. *J. H. Meredith/Online Transport Archive*

Bottom right: The same setting, but it's surely worth taking another look at what might have transformed tram travel in London, had such facilities been widespread. Ex-Walthamstow 'E1' No 2057 on a short working of route 16/18 to Norbury, with an ex-Croydon 'E1' going all the way to Purley behind. In the distance is a Central London-bound ex-LCC 'E1'. The date is 24 April 1948. *J. H. Meredith/Online Transport Archive*

and its number 92 (in London this would have been a West Ham 'E1'; I'm afraid I have no knowledge of Ilkley trams) – he would look up and declare: 'Eeeh, where did that low bridge come from?' and advise lady passengers: 'Don't go upstairs, they've gone, heee!' In a 1957 *Hancock's Half Hour* our hero, having been asked to present the prizes at his old public school, reminiscences on the career choices open to him when he was a pupil, one being tram driver. This surprises Sid James, but Tony comments that being able to call out the destination in Latin, 'Elephantus et Castella', for example, might have raised the tone of tram travel. There seems to be some confusion between the duties of driver and conductor. Driving a tram is a family tradition; as his mother, Hattie Jacques, explains, it was just a pity his father's career as such was brought to premature end when an inspector leapt on one day and asked why none of the passengers had been issued with tickets. It all ends disastrously when Sid tries to steal the prizes and headmaster Kenneth Williams reveals that the seven years Hancock spent as the school were as 'the worst porter we ever employed'.

Three years after the last trams passed through Brixton Bruce Forsyth appeared at the Empress, halfway down the bill with the tag line 'The Incredible Character'. The theatre was demolished in 1992 and replaced by a block of dull-looking flats.

The Brixton Theatre opened in 1896 with 'Mr Wilson Barrett sustaining the role of Marcus Superbus', which, one gathers, was not a remarkably prescient drama about the Borismaster but a Roman epic. The theatre was destroyed in the Blitz, on the night of 8 November 1940. Next door was the Ritz Cinema, dating from 1911, which survived (as did the Tate Library on the other side) and now occupies part of the theatre site.

Brixton has a pretty fair claim to be the most ethnically diverse community anywhere in the UK. Only recently my wife and I were sitting in the open-air café

Top: The top of Brixton Hill, and the boundary between Streatham and Brixton. One of the original Green Line AEC Regal coaches, T86 of 1930, on its way to Redhill, has made a possibly unscheduled stop outside Brixton tram depot, various bus, and possibly tram, men being clustered around it. Alongside is 'E1' tram No 1236 of 1910 vintage on route 10, behind is a Tilling ST on route 59, whilst heading towards Central London is a Tilling STL, both buses being from Croydon (TC) garage. It is clearly a warm summer's day – note the white-top hats and the windows of the 'E1', wound right down. T86 was withdrawn in 1938 – the same year that the 'E1' was fitted with windscreens; the tram would succumb in 1946. The first 'Felthams' arrived at Brixton and Telford Avenue depots, which worked route 10, in the winter of 1936/7, displacing ex-LCC 'E1s', and as all these had gone (either moved elsewhere or scrapped) by the summer of 1938 this picture could well have been taken during the summer of 1936. *London Transport*

Middle: Pursuing a Ford Prefect, 'Feltham' No 2133 on route 16 begins its descent of Brixton Hill *c*1949, whilst alongside a Standard Vanguard an 'E3' on route 18 is about to breast the summit, opposite Brixton depot. The Vanguard was part of a new, postwar generation of British-built saloons much influenced by transatlantic styling and was much used by the RAF. *B. J. Cross Collection/Online Transport Archive*

Bottom: Another top-of-Brixton Hill scene *c*1949. In this picture 'Feltham' No 2123 is working a rush-hour extra to Croydon, followed by an 'E3' on route 10 bound for Tooting, whilst a second 'Feltham' is just beginning the descent towards Lambeth Town Hall. *B. J. Cross Collection/Online Transport Archive*

… "What, an open-air café in Brixton?!" a time-traveller from the 1940s might be expected to exclaim. Please don't interrupt; yes, since you ask, opposite Lambeth Town Hall. Anyhow, she wandered over to a plaque on a wall close to where the Orange Luxury Coaches used to set off for the seaside and she was about to read when two coloured lads on bicycles, *à la* Bradley Wiggins, all bright-eyed and bushy-tailed, came peddling up and said, 'That's all about the Windrush, the ship that brought the first black people to England.'

A less entertaining architectural feature, easily seen if one looked to the left halfway down Brixton Hill, was the prison; still there, it is a pretty horrible place. It was built in 1820 as the Surrey House of Correction, and the following year the lucky inmates were provided with a tread wheel to keep them occupied. By the middle of the 19th century there were some 880 prisoners, including women, some of whom had opted to be sent there rather than be transported to Australia; many had babies with them. A number of reports in more recent times have been severely critical of conditions; one governor was dismissed, prisoner officers went on strike, and there was an inquiry into the large number of suicides, and although of late things would seem to have got better, with a governor who appears to have a real understanding of how people get dragged into criminality, the place is still said to be infested with vermin.

Two railway bridges spanned the tracks through central Brixton, the first, upon initial acquaintance seeming of great height (albeit less so today), whilst the other, come the 1990s, would see a regular service of electric trains running over it non-stop between Waterloo and Paris and Brussels. Not even the wildest of our schoolboy predictions of the future came up with that. We sometimes alighted from our 16 or 18 at Brixton and boarded (if I had my way, which I usually did in this respect), another 'Feltham' on the 8. This would take us past Pride & Clarke's motor-cycle emporium, under Vauxhall station and onto Vauxhall Bridge, with its view of Westminster. A straight run across Vauxhall Bridge meant the tram had been allowed to penetrate something like a mile into the West End. Six routes terminated at Victoria, which really could claim to serve the West End proper, for but a few yards away were

Below: Brixton town centre *c*1928, with two LCC 'E1' trams – No 1547 on the 78 and No 1172 on the 20. Behind are two London General K types and, almost out of the picture on the left, an NS with covered top. *Lambeth Libraries*

Above: The view south from Brixton town centre *c*1949, with tram No 2 working the 78 and, further along Effra Road, a 'prewar' RT (with distinctive roof-mounted rear number box) on the 37, passing a Bedford OB/Duple coach pulling out of the Orange Luxury coach station. *Lambeth Libraries*

Below: 'E3' No 1996 and 'camelback' LT909 in what must surely be a posed picture at the Effra Road, Brixton, changeover from pole to conduit. Note the inspectors – there seemed to be an awful lot of them about anyhow in those days (*c*1946) – and the white stripes on the pole left over from wartime. *Lambeth Libraries*

Buckingham Palace Road and Victoria Street, the Roman Catholic Cathedral and the Victoria Palace Theatre, which was home to those 'Kings of Comedy' the Crazy Gang, and where I once saw them perform the play scene, straight, from *A Midsummer Night's Dream*, which had the audience literally aching with laughter.

Kennington did – does – have its places of entertainment, notably The Oval, home of Surrey Cricket Club since 1845 and, after Lords, perhaps the best-known cricket ground in the world, set alongside its almost as famous gasholders, which date from 1853, but it is also a great place for churches. St John the Divine, dating from 1871-4, which could be seen, if you were quick, as your tram passed Vassall Road, in which it stands, is the work of George Edward Street (who designed the Royal Courts of Justice in the City) and was notably described by John Betjeman as 'the most magnificent church in South London'.

Another church, St Mark's, on the corner of Clapham Road and Kennington Oval, has several claims to fame and could not be missed, for it stood at the junction of the 2, 2A, 4, 4A, 4X, 6, 48 and 58 routes and within sight of the 10, 16, 16X, 18, 18X, 22, 24, 40 and 72. It was known as the 'Tramwayman's church', because so many employees and their families worshipped there, whilst the intersection outside was known as 'the Clapham Junction of the Southern roads' on account of the plethora of tram points and crossings. Bombed during the Blitz in 1940, the church was a sad-looking place, with only the façade, pillars and cupola still standing – just. Its priest, the Rev John Darlington, who used to wear top hat and tails on his way to worship, died in 1947 sadly expecting what remained to be demolished, but the Diocese of Southwark changed its mind, and it was rebuilt in 1960.

Routes 2 and 4, which came down Balham High Road and

Top: Brixton has always been one of the most cosmopolitan, bustling sorts of places within the inner-London suburbs. It certainly was on the day in the mid-1930s when this picture was taken. Most of the pedestrians seem to be crossing under the control of lights, but the smartly dressed mother and daughter, complete with regulation period headgear, are taking their chances ahead of ST255 on its way to the heart of the West End and beyond to Golders Green. This was something denied the trams – penetrating the heart of the West End, that is, not adopting smart headgear – although the 'E3' working route 33 will do its best, emerging in 18 minutes from the Kingsway Subway within a few hundred yards of Oxford Street and High Holborn. Behind it is an 'E1', while passing it is a Tilling ST heading south. The two railway bridges, high and low, are another indication of how well served Brixton was (and is) by public transport, although it would be some decades before the Tube reached Brixton, and it is doubtful whether any of those bustling pedestrians can ever have envisaged a time when surface trains would run through Brixton non-stop *en route* to Paris or Brussels. *London Transport Collection*

Middle: Either the climate has changed, permanently, or the population has loosened up considerably since the 1930s, and one suspects it's the latter, for who would have thought of pavement cafés in Brixton back then?

Left: 'Feltham' No 2145 heads south along Brixton Road, which links Kennington with Brixton, on its way to Croydon and Purley *c*1948. Many of the large, late-Victorian houses, which would have started out with front gardens, most probably tended by professional gardeners, have now seen these turned over to tarmac, sporting some choice examples of the motor-car designer's art.

through Stockwell to join us, and I were old friends, although, being worked exclusively by 'E1s', they were, in my eyes, of somewhat inferior status. We had first met at Wimbledon, where the trams shared a terminus with the 604 and 605 trolleybuses but which I usually reached by way of the ancient two-coach electric trains which ran over surprisingly rural, mostly single track from West Croydon (which would, in the fullness of time, bring trams back to Wimbledon.) We met again at Tooting Broadway, where the line was crossed by the only London trolleybus route I used regularly, the 630 from West Croydon to 'Near Willesden Junction' (or, as far as I was concerned, the bridge over the GWR main line out of Paddington at Old Oak Common) and then again, a mile or so further on, at Balham station, through which decidedly insecure-looking wooden structure I would pass in my train to Victoria.

From the far east, from Greenwich and Woolwich, both of which I knew from our annual expedition by paddle-steamer from Tower Pier to Southend (from Grove Park, which was almost Bromley – where lived ancient aunts – but not quite), and from Forest Hill, where the 66s met the 194 buses which to used to convey me to cricket, rugby and cross-country at Sandilands, in Shirley (where Tramlink now operates), came hordes of 'E1s', many of them housed at New Cross, London's largest tram depot, with a capacity of 314 cars. It would prove to be the tram's last stronghold, and there were many, albeit very much in a minority, who bravely tried to hold back the abolitionist tide and argued that the tram was peculiarly suited to the southeast suburbs, badly served as they were by the Underground. Few wished to retain the fleet of 'E1s' or the rather more modern but still outdated 'E3s' and 'HR2s', but plans, pictures and statistics relating to the modern American single-deck PCC cars or their European derivatives then in production provided evidence that the tram had a future. Such vehicles did indeed ensure the survival of the tram (or streetcar) until the long-hoped-for worldwide revival became a reality as the 21st century approached. I always kept a lookout in the hope that I might spot one of

Above: St John the Divine, Kennington, designed by George Edward Street and completed in 1874, described by John Betjeman as 'the most magnificent church in South London'.

Below: This view of the north side of Vauxhall station, recorded *c*1910, serves to emphasise the dominance of the tram in its Edwardian heyday. All the cars are either 'Es' or 'E1s'.

Above: 16s crossing at Kennington on 24 July 1948. Nearer the camera is an Embankment-bound ex-LCC 'E3', whilst approaching is an ex-Croydon Corporation 'E1'. *B. T. Cooke*

Below: St Mark's Church, Kennington, known as the 'tramwayman's church' and situated at one of the busiest tram intersections in London. One of the short-lived, if long-limbed, Mercedes bendi-buses heads across the junction towards Victoria in the summer of 2011. St Mark's was badly damaged in the Blitz and stood derelict for many years, finally being restored in 1960. *B. T. Cooke/B. J. Cross Collection*

the pair of much modified 'ME3' cars (or No 2, a heavily rebuilt 'E1'), with their domed roofs, roller-blind indicators and other improvements, which, along with No 1 and the 'Felthams', were the only London trams which could truly be described as modern.

For a seemingly fairly ordinary inner-London suburb Kennington, described in Somerset Maugham's *Of Human Bondage* as a district of 'vulgar respectability', has had a quite extraordinary collection of residents over the years. These range from Captain Bligh of the *Bounty*, the artist William Blake, William Booth, founder of the Salvation Army, Vincent van Gogh (Christ Church, which in itself is a wonderful building, on the A23 has a 'Vincent van Gogh' café), Charlie Chaplin and Field Marshall Bernard Montgomery to, in more modern times, Bob Marley, James Callaghan, who as Prime Minister had to be persuaded to leave his flat there for 10 Downing Street, Kenneth Clarke, the inimitable Max Wall, who had the funniest legs in Christendom (eat your heart out, John Cleese), and Kevin Spacey. In fact Kennington, in common with just about every suburb, is full of surprises. Only a few days ago, when travelling along Kennington Road on a 159 bus (which the 159s

Above: Ex-Walthamstow 'E1' No 2054, of New Cross depot, at Kennington Gate on 22 September 1951. There would appear to be no fewer than three Morris 10 saloons in the picture – one heading the same way as No 2054, one behind the Harrington-bodied coach, with its distinctive dorsal fin, and the third a little further on, on the same side of the road, being overtaken by an RT and with a cyclist about to follow suit.
J. H. Meredith/Online Transport Archive

have always done, originally having to squeeze between the trams working routes 2, 2A, 2X, 4, 4A, 4X, 16, 16X, 18, 18X, 22 and 24) I was reminded how remarkably leafy it is, just as it was when Charlie Chaplin walked it, not being able to afford the tram fare, like the tramp-like figures he observed doing the same thing.

Almost there now. Waterloo comes next. The London & South Western Railway would have liked to extend its line across the river into the City, but around 1850 the City Fathers calculated that, if all the proposed stations had been allowed, over one quarter of its territory would have been covered by railway line. Thus the LSWR had to be content with a station at what was originally entitled Waterloo Road, which grew and grew in such a haphazard manner that, in the words of Jerome K. Jerome, 'nobody at Waterloo ever knows where a train is going to start from, or a train when it does start is going to.' The best that could be done was to construct a Tube line, the Waterloo & City (or, as it would come to be known, 'The Drain'), to the Bank of England. Tram lines duly arrived, and whilst those on the east side, in Waterloo Road, did not continue across Waterloo Bridge, those on the west side, used by trams from Croydon,

dived under the platforms, and upon emerging and passing St Thomas's Hospital on their left and County Hall on their right travellers thereon would find themselves on Westminster Bridge, confronted with one of the most celebrated views in Christendom, the Houses of Parliament seen from across the River Thames.

Across the bridge, whilst buses were allowed into Parliament Square and up Whitehall, trams found themselves banished to the Embankment, built in the 1850s by Joseph Bazalgette on behalf of the Metropolitan Board of Works as part of a sewerage-relief system and also to relieve traffic elsewhere – which, possibly more by accident than design, created a tram-spotter's heaven through which, during the busiest periods, around 100 trams would pass during the course of an hour.

Above: The Wimbledon terminus of routes 2 and 4, which were worked by elderly 'E1s' from Clapham depot. This picture would seem to date from late 1938 or early 1939, for in the background is 'K1' trolleybus No 1102, which was not delivered from Leyland until November 1938. It is working from Fulwell depot on the 604 – a most unusual occurrence, for this was normally the exclusive preserve of the original LUT 'Diddlers', and indeed No 1102 would soon be moved elsewhere. 'E1' No 1530 of 1911 is working route 2, while No 1777, the first of the 1922 batch, not yet fitted with windscreens (which it would gain in July 1939), is working the 4. *A. W. V. Mace*

Above: The Café Van Gogh in Brixton Road, Kennington. In 1873 the young Vincent lived just around the corner, in Hackford Road, where, apparently, he fell in love with his landlady's daughter.

Left: The 68 was the only regular route to terminate beside Waterloo station, but if you were very lucky you might just come across the 36EX or the 38EX – but only, believe it or not, on Easter, Whitsun or August bank holidays! Here, in April 1951, passengers alight from one of the final, 1930-vintage 'E1s'. The Old Vic theatre is in the background (right). *Pamlin Prints*

Above: The Embankment c1937, this being the view eastwards towards Blackfriars. A Leyland lorry is slightly ahead of one of the original Green Line Ts of 1929/30, various private-hire coaches are parked with their backs to the camera, and the only tram in evidence is an 'HR2' on route 62. *London Transport*

Below: 'Felthams' on routes 20 and 22 pass in South Lambeth Road on 6 November 1951. Heading for Victoria, on the left, is No 2135, whilst southbound is No 2128. Both went to Leeds, but, by an odd coincidence, neither entered service there. *J. H. Meredith/Online Transport Archive*

Above: Men at work on Vauxhall Bridge c1950. Waiting patiently to continue on its way to Victoria is 'Feltham' No 2132, with an 'HR2' behind. The star of the scene is a 4-ton Leyland Cub SKZ1, an example the LPTB's first standard lorry, one of 29 such vehicles dating from 1936, this particular one being equipped for tramway track welding. It shared its CXX registration series with STLs and '9T9' and Q-type Green Line coaches. *B. J. Cross Collection/Online Transport Archive*

Left: The view south across Westminster Bridge towards St Thomas' Hospital. 'E3' No 1920, on its way to Hackney by way of the Kingsway Subway, is followed by an 'E1' on route 26, another 'E3' northbound on route 35 to Archway and finally a rehabilitated 'E1'. *A. W. V. Mace*

Right: One of the few places in the West End to be reached by trams was Victoria. Pictured in 1949, 'E3' No 1862 stands at the Vauxhall Bridge Road terminus of the 54, shared with routes 8, 20, 28, 58 and 78. Immediately beyond is a much-appreciated refreshment stall, whilst across Victoria Street is the Victoria Palace, for many years home to the Crazy Gang. *A. W. V. Mace*

Below: A photograph taken at the same location some 12 years earlier. 'E1' No 1627 is working circular route 20 to Tooting via Brixton and Streatham; behind is 'E1' No 1092, also bound for Tooting but in the reverse direction via Clapham and Balham. No 1627 was fitted with windscreens in December 1938 and withdrawn in May 1951, No 1092 being so equipped in March 1938 and withdrawn in February 1951. By 1938, a year or so after this picture was taken, 'Felthams' were sharing the 8 and 20 with the 'E1s', which did nothing to enhance the reputation of these ex-LCC cars. *A. W. V. Mace*

9

FURTHER TRAVELS THROUGH SUBURBIA

'E1' No 1747 heads along the Embankment towards London Bridge. However, unlike the 70 the 26 terminated west of the station, at the Hop Exchange – a reminder that at this time thousands of East Enders took a working holiday picking hops in the Kent hop fields, which they could reach by train from London Bridge. There was no connection between the two tram termini. *A. W. V. Mace*

Our local route 42 was, I later came to realise, all but unique in that by 1948 practically all tram routes reached Central London, the only other I can recall that didn't being the 44. This connected Woolwich with Eltham, although why it was necessary at all when the 46 covered exactly the same territory, having hardly got into its stride at Eltham before it got down to the serious business of heading through Lee Green, Lewisham, New Cross and past the Bricklayers Arms to the City end of Southwark Bridge, I cannot tell you. I only once made the journey to Southwark Bridge by tram. Each summer Great Aunt Hatt and I would make an expedition to London during her annual visit from Shropshire. Here, some 30 years earlier, she had helped bring up Mum, her mother, Aunt Hatt's sister, having died when she was a small child. I had once been rather frightened of her formidable aspect and manner, but I soon came to feel differently, and we became firm friends. I guess it would have been in 1947 that I persuaded her that we should travel to this exciting place I had seen displayed on route 10's trams, 'City and Southwark'. So we took either a 16 or 18 to Streatham Hill, where I insisted on getting off a stop too soon so that I could watch from ground level the change from overhead to conduit collection. I had often observed this from the upper deck of a tram and, looking down, had seen the inspector complete with braided cap (not sure how essential this was in the process) and fork-like instrument push the plough into the nether regions of the tram or, heading home in the opposite direction, much more excitingly had watched it come flying out and zoom on its own single track into the siding between the up and down tracks, sometimes giving a wallop to ploughs already there, stationary and minding their own business. It took me some while to work the system out. For a time I assumed the centre, conduit track was live, as on the Underground, but I soon realised that this might

cause certain problems. Mind you, as we had no electricity in our house (lighting being by gas, the wireless powered by an accumulator which I had to take round to the Victory garage at the Pond each week to have charged and collect its fellow, being careful – very careful – not to spill any of the acid) I never really understood the difference between watts, volts and ohms, although I quite quickly learned to tell live from dead.

Having walked up the hill to St Leonard's Church, in which I felt a certain proprietorial interest, Leonard being my father's name, and espied a 'Feltham' coming around the bend of Mitcham Lane and leapt aboard, whereupon the conductor rang the bell from upstairs, leaving Aunt Hatt behind. She valiantly ran alongside across the busy road junction, as I stood panic-stricken on the platform, but my great aunt was no match for the 'Feltham', and she dropped behind. I got off at the next stop, Aunt Hatt caught up, without recrimination, good soul that she was, and we boarded a former Walthamstow 'E1'.

I was allowed, with Aunt Hatt's money, to purchase the tickets, so I asked for one and a half to Southwark, pronouncing it phonetically as spelt. Aunt Hatt could hardly have been expected to get her head around the subtleties of the Cockney pronunciations, but fortunately the conductor understood my Thornton Heath accent, and we settled down for the journey, which was through familiar territory as far as the Elephant & Castle. This was just about the busiest junction on the entire London tram network, probably outdoing Kennington. A one-way system operated which took the 4s, 4As, 4Xs, 18s,

Right: 'Feltham' No 2138 at St Leonard's Church, about to swing down Streatham High Road on its way to Purley, c1949. The much larger Croydon was always given at least equal prominence on the 16/18 destination screen. Also in the picture are a Q-type single-decker, which is probably in use as a Green Line coach, and an Austin 8 saloon.

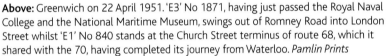

Above: Greenwich on 22 April 1951. 'E3' No 1871, having just passed the Royal Naval College and the National Maritime Museum, swings out of Romney Road into London Street whilst 'E1' No 840 stands at the Church Street terminus of route 68, which it shared with the 70, having completed its journey from Waterloo. *Pamlin Prints*

Right: An attractive LCC poster extolling the glories of Greenwich Park, although one wonders how many magnificent Landseer-type stags at bay one might expect to see from the upper deck of an 'E1'. *London Transport*

18Xs, 24s, 34s, 34Xs, 36s, 36Xs, 38Xs, 66s, 68s, 74s, 74Xs and 84s up St George's Road, whilst southbound the 2s, 2As, 2Xs, 16s, 22s, 35s, 36s, 38s, 38Xs, 56s, 62s, 66s, 66Xs, 68s, 74s, 74Xs, and 84s came down London Road. Our 10, along with the 6s, 48s and 60s, headed up Borough (I got the pronunciation of that right) High Street. At the next junction, where Great Dover Street met Marshalsea Street (straight out of Dickens!), if trams had ever been allowed to continue they would have arrived at the terminus of the 12, 14 and 26 beside Southwark Cathedral or across on the far side of London Bridge station, down in Tooley Street, where the 70 had a terminus all to itself. Trams never were allowed to cross London Bridge and enter the City proper; fortunately the unfashionable Borough of Southwark was not so fussy.

The 70 led a rather lonely existence, sharing most of its route with the 68 through Rotherhithe, past the Surrey Docks, along Creek Road and Bridge Street to Greenwich, but otherwise meeting no other trams until its Greenwich terminus in Church Street. Tooley Street, beside London Bridge station, might hardly be thought to qualify as suburbia, but it was an area as remote as

one could imagine from the grand buildings and aspirations on the north bank of the Thames. The 70 and the 68 passed through an area dominated by the London Docks, where there was grinding poverty, where dockers got paid only when they worked (which depended upon whether there were ships to load or unload), and where many of the houses were defined as slums – those, that is, which hadn't been bombed out of existence. Working on the docks could be hazardous. Uncle Harry, who lived in leafy Sanderstead, on the slopes of the North Downs, and who travelled up each day through London Bridge station on his way to his office in Fenchurch Street, where he was an executive with the Union Castle shipping line, once, whilst crossing London Bridge, saw a heavy packing case slip from its sling and crush to death the stevedore who had been standing beneath it. Much later, in the early 1970s, one of my fellow teachers at Oxted County School (on the other, even more leafy side of the North Downs from Sanderstead), was Ed, who was in charge of metalwork and had been brought up in Rotherhithe in the late 1920s and '30s. He was a lovely man, who had great sympathy for the 15-year-old hard cases who were condemned to spend most of the their time in the metalwork, woodwork and art departments when what they needed most was a crash course in basic literacy and numeracy, and had become a teacher at the insistence of his stevedore father, who told him the last thing he needed was a son to follow in his footsteps. Nowadays I find that part of London fascinating and rather romantic, especially when I poke about to see if I can find any reminders of tram days, not to say travelling on the wonderful Docklands Light Railway, serving Greenwich, Lewisham and Woolwich, which is halfway to being a tram system, but I have only to recall Ed talking about the 'good old days' to remove my rose-tinted spectacles.

Back to Aunt Hatt and my expedition on the 10. It was a route which as I recall passed under a number of railway bridges, carrying the lines to Waterloo, Charing Cross, Cannon Street, Blackfriars and Holborn Viaduct stations, all extremely busy, although all had also suffered a decline some 40 years earlier, due, in part, to the newly electrified tram routes' stealing some of their business. At Southwark Bridge Road we made our last turn, due north, and crossed Southwark Street, which carried the 12 and 26 trams eastward to their London Bridge terminus (a different one from Tooley Street, this being termed Southwark Street, Borough); westward these headed to Wandsworth and Clapham Junction, although they had once gone further, the 12 to Tooting, the 26 to Kew Bridge, having been cut back when trolleybuses arrived in 1937 to share their Wandsworth depot. We headed along Marshalsea Road, the notorious prison of that name now but a disturbing memory. Charles Dickens' father was twice imprisoned in the Marshalsea for debt. The Dickens family were lucky in that the first time a legacy secured their release; the second time young Charles himself paid off his spendthrift's father's debt. But many never came out, dying there of starvation. The memory of this so

seared into his memory that again and again Dickens drew upon the experience in his novels, and this did much to hasten prison reform. One wall survives, and the local history museum, fittingly, is there. Dickens wrote the prison's epitaph, a masterpiece of understatement – 'It is gone now, and the world is no worse for it.' Proceeding along Southwark Bridge Road, we came out above the river with that always wonderful view, upstream to Blackfriars railway bridge, downstream to Cannon Street railway bridge and London Bridge with the Pool of London beyond, ships tied up on both banks, many being unloaded into lighters (barges) to be taken further upriver, whilst on this particular morning it was possible to see the upper works of the passenger ferry on the City side, close to London Bridge, about to cast off on its regular twice-weekly voyage across the North Sea to Rotterdam; visible between its masts was Tower Bridge. And so our journey ended beside the gaunt, bomb-damaged outline of Cannon Street station – my one and only tram ride within the City of London, if only for a few yards. Route 10 shared this terminus with the 6, 46 and 48, and if we waited until the rush hour we'd also encounter 52s and 60s. Southwark was (and remains) the least used of all the Central London road bridges, and it was possible to stand in the road and note somewhat smugly that the 10 was the only service which employed 'Felthams', the rest having to make do with 'E1s' and 'E3s'.

Right: A crowded Pool of London c1930, with a well-loaded paddle-steamer of the General Steam Navigation Co setting off for Southend.

Left: Viewed from the nearside front seat of an RT near Deptford, windswept passengers board 'E1' No 916 on route 68 on a blustery, grey day *c*1949. Beyond the gaunt trees is a bombsite, not yet redeveloped.

Below: Recently rehabilitated 'E1' No 978 gingerly negotiates road works in Lewisham. In the distance are two Tilling STs, belonging either to Catford or Bromley garage. The tar boiler with its tall chimney, bearing a passing resemblance to a very early railway locomotive, was a familiar sight in the streets of London well into postwar years, although this photograph would have been taken *c*1938. *A. W. V. Mace*

Above: One of the final batch of 1930-vintage 'E1s' at the Tooley Street terminus of route 70 on the north side of London Bridge station – a route which served the heart of Docklands south of the river, passing within a few hundred yards of Tower Bridge, continuing on through Bermondsey, the Surrey Docks, Deptford, Creek Road and Bridge Street – the names tell all – before terminating in Greenwich. *A. W. V. Mace*

Left: Pictured c1950, 'E3' No 1932 has just passed St Leonard's Church, Streatham, and is heading along Mitcham Lane towards Mitcham and Tooting; in the distance is a 'Feltham'. 'E3s' were not normally seen here, the usual fare being ex-LCC and ex-Walthamstow 'E1s' – plus, of course, the 'Felthams'.

10

GO NORTHWEST, YOUNG MAN

Rehabilitated 'E1' No 1384 in Queen's Road, Battersea, in 1950, its terminus having been cut back from the King's Road, Chelsea, by the temporary closure of Battersea Bridge. On the other side of the traffic island is a Duple-bodied Bedford OB, far and away the most popular coach and rural bus of the immediate postwar years.

There were a couple of other tram-related journeys which I made as a child, never on my own but with parents and other relations. These were to Hampton Court and Kew Gardens. I say tram-related because the trams which would have conveyed me, had I been born a few years earlier, had by now gone, replaced by trolleybuses. It is just possible that I met a route-30 tram, for I was three months old when the 630 trolleybus took over, but I very much doubt if I would have travelled on one. The 30 terminated in Tamworth Road, West Croydon, and officially there was no connection with the lines used by routes 16, 18 and 42 which crossed at right-angles a few yards distant. However, I was pretty sure that as a very small child I had seen a section of rail sticking out of the road surface at this junction curving from Tamworth Road towards the London Road. Childhood recollections can certainly not be relied upon; but I was very pleased to discover, years later, that there had indeed been such a connection, a single track, never used by passenger-carrying cars but which enabled trams based at Thornton Heath depot to take up work on the 30. Generally when trams ceased running the tracks would be taken up almost immediately, but, depending on the current price of scrap, they might be left in place and covered with tarmac, so that it remained possible for years afterwards to detect their ghostly presence lurking below, until, as if auditioning for a part in a tram-based horror film, a small section would gradually reappear. In the last years of route 30's existence the ramshackle ex-South Met cars had been replaced by former LCC 'E'-class trams, and those in turn by 'E1s', which would have been an improvement, although none had driver's windscreens.

We would board the 630, although not usually at its West Croydon terminus. This was beyond that of the 30 tram but situated more conveniently in Station Road, where a number of bus routes, including Country Area services, also terminated and where a turning-loop was provided. We would walk down the A23 Thornton Road to where the Mitcham Road crossed it. A couple of stops further on we passed Aurelia Road, in which the one-time

Above: The more southerly of the two changeover points for route 30 was in Tooting, between Amen Corner and the Broadway. A few days before the 630 trolleybuses took over (on 12 September 1937) the conductor of an 'E1' does a balancing act as he prepares to lower the pole. Clearly, judging by the open windows upstairs, summer had not yet departed.

South Met depot, which supplied some of the trams for the 30, was situated. This had closed in November 1937. Decades later Tramlink would site its depot at Therapia Lane, just across Mitcham Road from Aurelia Road.

The wide open spaces of Mitcham Common gave enterprising (or daredevil) trolleybus drivers the opportunity to put on speed. Perhaps tram drivers – one and the same in the early days, no doubt – had also put their feet down, although the 'Es', dating from 1906 and, unlike the 'E1s', never fitted with more-powerful motors, were not noted for overdoing things in this respect. The evocatively named Fair Green at Mitcham was a bit of a let-down, being neither fair nor green – unlike Mitcham Cricket Green, just up the road, which was and is a delightful spot, a one-time tram terminus, bounded by houses and cottages long preceding any form of transport other than that drawn by a horse and with a real cricket pitch separated from the pavilion by a bus route (surely unique?). The Fair Green was, until September 1937, the terminus of tram routes 6 and 12 – and, on Sunday afternoons (after church), the 31.

None actually disappeared at this date, the 6 being cut back to Tooting Amen Corner, a mile or distant, the 12 and 31 to Wandsworth. Trolleybus 612 replaced the Mitcham–Tooting section of the 12. [1006]

Amen Corner – how did it get that name? It was certainly there long before the pop group of that name was formed in the 1960s, the founder of which lived nearby; most likely it was because a church once stood on the spot. Whatever, it was seen as a suitable terminus for the 6, and it until January 1951 it continued to be served by no fewer than six other tram routes – the 1, 8, 10, 20, 22 and 24, which came in along Southcroft Road from Streatham. I never encountered all-night service 1, being safely tucked up in bed before it ventured out, from its Clapham and Telford Avenue depots. The latter depot shared the 8 and 20 with Clapham and the 10 with Brixton Hill, while Clapham also worked the 22 and the 24. I used to feel sorry for the citizens of Clapham, as their depot housed nothing but 'E1s', most of them well past their sell-by date, although they had the consolation that if they waited a 'Feltham' would also come along on the 8 or the 20.

Tooting Broadway was sheer heaven for enthusiasts of electrically powered transport. Down below was the

Above: Tooting Broadway c1948. Passengers are alighting from an 'E1' on its way from Wimbledon to the Embankment, while a trolleybus working either the 628 or the 630 is about to cross the Broadway from Mitcham Road into Garratt Lane. The track curving around to the right, from the High Street into Mitcham Road, is clearly no longer in use.

Northern Line station, and through it passed the latest Tube trains, the iconic 1938 stock, on their way to or from Morden, whilst up above the 'E1s' (which I suppose could once have been so described) operating the 2 and 4 tram routes came in from Wimbledon and joined all the others which had shared our 612/630 road, and which now swung due north, joining the 2s and 4s on their way to Balham ('Gateway to the South', to quote the Peter Sellers, Frank Muir and Denis Norden travelogue spoof, with its dazzling illuminations turning from red through amber to green), Clapham Common and Stockwell. Our 630, in company with the 612, made its way northwestwards along Garratt Lane, past Wimbledon Stadium and a mile or so distant from the All England Lawn Tennis Club at Wimbledon (the 1947 champions were Jack Kramer and Margaret duPont, both from the USA), to a final tram meeting, at Wandsworth. Here terminated the 12 and the 31, both of which had once worked alongside tram route 30 from Mitcham. The 31 was a reminder of how different the London tram scene might have been, had not the powers that be been so adamant in their refusal to allow trams through the West End, for it connected Wandsworth, Battersea and with Bloomsbury and Clerkenwell and The Angel, Islington, by way of the Kingsway Subway.

Wandsworth, so named for it is here that Croydon's own River Wandle (Tramlink traverses Wandle Park) enters the Thames, is mentioned in Domesday. Clapham Junction, a tram terminus as well as the UK's busiest through railway station, is actually in Wandsworth, but its builders felt that Clapham sounded more upmarket. Much of South West London was served by Wandsworth Gasworks, the coal for which was brought up the river by barge, but it was probably most famous for its brewery, the oldest in England, owned by Young's, which still has its headquarters here, although brewing finished in 2005. Among the transport delights were the two beautifully turned-out horse drays, which were still at work delivering beer into the 21st century.

Crossing the Thames at Putney Bridge, we would enter Fulham and have the opportunity if we were on the upper deck (where else?) to peer over the wall into the grounds of Fulham Palace. We might be somewhat surprised to find extensive allotments, which were not there to keep the Bishop occupied Monday to Saturday but had been established during the war for local people to supplement their rations and in 1948 were still very much in use, there seemingly being little likelihood of rationing come to an end in the immediate future. But we would have left trams behind for good now, although 10 years earlier the 26, the 26X, the 28 and the 30 ran here and at Hammersmith Broadway met the 67 and the 89. The 67, to Hampton Court, had been one of the very first conversions under London Transport, in October 1935, becoming the 667 trolleybus route, worked by Fulwell depot. This was home to London's

Above: An evocative night scene recorded *c*1939 at Tooting Broadway, with a 'Feltham' and its driver awaiting custom on night route 1. *London Transport*

first production trolleybuses, the LUT 'Diddlers', which might sometimes, therefore, be seen on the 667, a route which could be become extremely busy on fine weekends. It was at Hammersmith that I first saw a 'Diddler', a year before they were all withdrawn. I thought it both extremely antiquated and ugly, with its protruding snout, peaks over both lower- and upper-deck front windows and upright stance. I took an awful lot of convincing that it emanated from the same stable as the beautiful 'Felthams' and, indeed, resembled them in certain aspects.

Right: An ex-LCC 'E' type negotiates the temporary track at the northern end of Mitcham Common, in use while the railway bridge was being rebuilt. Shortly afterwards, in 1937, the 30's trams would be replaced by trolleybuses on route 630.

Left: A pair of ex-Leyton Corporation 'E3s', Nos 196 and 198, at the Wandsworth High Street terminus of route 12 c1949.

Below: 'E1' No 1797 swings around the corner of Merton Road on a short working of route 2 to Stockwell c1950, pursued by a Citroën Light 15 and partially obscuring a station wagon of transatlantic origin.

Above: An 'E3' on route 12 crosses the railway tracks outside Nine Elms goods depot c1947.

Below: Clapham Junction. Rail grinder No 015 climbs Lavender Hill on a damp, wintry afternoon c1949, passing a parked Bradford van and heading a Series E Morris 8 saloon and a wartime D-type Daimler of Merton garage on route 77, with an STL patiently bringing up the rear. No 015 had been rebuilt in 1930 from No 273, a Brush LCC open-top four-wheeler of 1906.

Above: Clapham Junction in 1937, shortly after trolleybuses had brought to an end route 26's excursions over the river to Hammersmith and Kew Bridge, the 'Junction' being now its western terminus. On the opposite side of the road a new 'E3' trolleybus has just arrived from Craven Park on route 628, which replaced tram route 28.

Below: Pursued by an STL working from Victoria garage, a rehabilitated 'E1' heads along Lavender Hill c1949, passing a gap left by a Nazi bomb in the line of substantial villas.

Left: Putney Bridge in Edwardian times. The LCC tram – either an 'E' or an 'E1' – heading south on route 1 from Harlesden to Putney (and almost at its terminus) looks vastly more modern than anything else negotiating the bridge. Prominent on the north bank is All Saints', Fulham, the tower of which dates from 1440, the rest rebuilt by that prolific Victorian church architect, Sir Arthur Blomfield. The picture is taken from the tower of St Mary's, Putney, an even older church; Putney was and is unique in being the only bridge over the Thames with a church at either end.

Below: An ex-LUT 'T' type on Putney Bridge. Although renumbered 2352 and bearing its new owner's lettering the tram is still in LUT livery, so the date must be 1933. There were 40 of the 'T' type, built by the United Electric Car Co of Preston in 1906. They had covered tops from new, but the windscreens, not fitted to all the members, were a 1920s addition. The cars lasted until 1936. *B. J. Cross Collection/Online Transport Archive*

Above: Hammersmith Broadway *c*1932. Centre-stage is 'Bluebird' LT1313 working route 11, on the far left 'E1' No 1045 on route 28 from Scrubs Lane, Willesden (otherwise known as 'near Willesden Junction'), to Victoria. Trolleybuses would take over the Willesden–Wandsworth section of the 28 in September 1937. *London Transport*

Left: An LUT poster for Hampton Court, which was served by route 67 to Hammersmith and the 71 to Wimbledon. Between May 1926 and the introduction of trolleybuses in September 1931 LCC routes 2 and 4 were extended from Wimbledon to Hampton Court on summer Saturdays and Sundays, although it was said that LCC crews were not best pleased, as the track was in very poor condition. *London Transport*

Opposite top: The northwestern end of tram route 28 was replaced by trolleybus 628 which ran between Craven Park and Clapham Junction. Here No 753, the last of the all-Leyland 'F1' class dating from 1937, negotiates the eastern end of Shepherd's Bush ahead of No 1279, another all-Leyland of the slightly later 'K1' class of 1938.

Opposite bottom: Shepherd's Bush – a picture taken in October 1935, judging by the sticker on the lower panel announcing route 57's conversion to trolleybus operation, effected on the 27th of that month. No 2406 was an ex-LUT 'W' type. Dating from 1902, it was one of five such cars rebuilt with an enclosed (except for the end balconies) upper deck. Upon withdrawal it was scrapped at Hendon (later Colindale) depot. Remarkably, decades later three old tramcar bodies were found at Ewhurst Green in Surrey, one of them belonging to 'W' type No 159, and today this can once again be seen running, at the National Tramway Museum at Crich. *B. J. Cross Collection/Online Transport Archive*

11

TOWARDS THE END

Two 'E3s' at Holborn station in the Kingsway Subway. *A. W. V. Mace*

Saddened as I was by the removal in April 1951 of the trams which passed the end of our road, when I started to put this book together I wondered briefly why I hadn't made more of an effort to travel on the remaining parts of the network until it all came to an end the following July – until I remembered that I was financially dependent on pocket money, which certainly wouldn't have stretched to journeys all over South London. I did once attempt to cycle northeastwards to try to make contact with the Downham trams, which lasted until January 1952, but without a map and with the wind against me I got hopelessly lost and gave up. My only subsequent tram ride in London (well, until the year 2000), was the one and only time I managed a trip in the Kingsway Subway, which I achieved just before its last route, the 33, succumbed on 5 April 1952.

Above: 'E3' No 1992 emerges from the north end of the Kingsway Subway, the jokey slogan chalked on its bumper indicating this is the very last day of the 33s and thus also the last day when it will be possible to see a tram heading for a destination which sounds like something out of *The Goon Show*.

Although the tidal wave which was, seemingly inexorably, sweeping away every tram network in the UK had been briefly (if entirely inadvertently) held back by Nazi hordes, there were those who fought it, not simply by appealing to nostalgia but with reasoned argument. The leading campaigner for the retention of trams in London was Alan Watkins. A member of the Light Railway Transport League, he was tireless in writing to local and national newspapers, MPs, London Transport, local authorities and anyone who had influence and who would listen to him. Many others also campaigned, particularly for the retention of Kingsway Subway and the routes in South East London, where Underground and Tube railways were, with a couple of exceptions, conspicuous by their absence. One letter to the *Kentish Independent*, a paper which was rather sympathetic to tramway retention, pointed out that to build a tunnel for trams would cost a tenth of that for a Tube railway – although just how the writer arrived at this somewhat surprising conclusion was not explained, but the suggestion was that trams could run in tunnels in congested town and city centres and 'come to the surface where there is sufficient room and run on lines fenced off from adjacent roads'.

The success of the American PCC streetcar and its European derivative, which, like the 'Feltham', represented a complete rethink of the street-railway vehicle, was frequently alluded to. If London were to have a new generation of trams they should be single-deck and one-man-operated, tickets being bought before boarding or from machines, while raised boarding platforms would obviate the need for passengers to walk out into the middle of the street. Nothing new under the sun there then. Its time would come.

To mark the end of the first generation of trams in London *The Economist* published an article entitled 'A Street Car named Defunct' and listed the following reasons for tramway abandonment:

- Trams were not allowed to run in the West End of London
- Prejudice against trams
- Very limited allowance of trams into the City
- With its narrow streets London was not like Continental cities
- 1870 Tramways Act, which stipulated that the road between the rails and pavement 18 inches either side had to be maintained by the operating powers
- Housing developments which were away from routes made tramway extension expensive
- Continental cities did not have the same amount of urban sprawl, hence tramways were economically viable

Above: The night-time crowd gathered around the changeover point at Effra Road, Brixton, strongly suggests that something out of the ordinary is going on, and it is very likely that this picture was taken on the final night of 33s, 5 April 1952.

Although the tram was generally regarded as old-fashioned and out of date, it nevertheless, right until the end, generated much interest from the public generally and a good deal of wry affection, whilst many writers were attracted to it. Writing in *The Observer* in 1950, Diana Gillon waxed lyrical: 'It will be hard for London's children when the trams are entirely demoded. Even an ordinary one, crashing its swaying way through suburb or provincial city, the crackling of electricity, the occasional thrilling spark, even this has charm that no mere bus can approach. And these miraculous Kingsway trams, which can plunge out of their proper element in the manner of an amphibian jeep, are obviously beyond compare … Still more impressive are the trams that emerge from the North. At first only far summer thunder, they are suddenly visible —a blinking eye in the darkness, piled background of illumination, and a gallant climb.'

The article ended with this thought: 'The tram is still a major form of transport in Europe, with the exception of France … yet there are signs on the Continent that the tram will go on for ever.' Today, of course, not only does it look as though the tram will go on for ever, but even France has embraced it, with probably more enthusiasm than anywhere else, opening an average of one new system every year. Would that the UK were prepared to fund public transport with the same generosity as the French.

But the tram had been doomed in the mid-1930s, and although the war had prolonged its life it had done nothing for maintenance standards. Mind you, it had done even less for much of the motor-bus fleet, and London Transport had first to get rid of all its tired, worn-out Regents inherited from the LGOC – and, indeed, some more modern STLs – before it could start removing the trams operating south of the Thames. The process began with Wandsworth's trams – and its trolleybuses, which must surely have sent a shiver down the poles of the rest of the fleet – on the night of 30 September/ 1 October 1950. The

Left: A scene from *The Elephant Will Never Forget*, the celebrated film made by London Transport to mark the passing of the first generation of London's trams. Although portrayed as husband and wife the jolly, elderly couple were not related and just happened to be sitting together. *London Transport*

process continued inexorably, the oldest trams, ex-LCC 'E1s', regardless of where they were based, being withdrawn and broken up first, so that by the final abandonment on the night of 5/6 July 1952 all that were left some ex-East Ham and West Ham 'E1s', No 2 and a fair number of 'HR2s' and 'E3s'.

Stan Collins was given the job of driving the last tram on our local route, from Norbury to Telford Avenue depot. This was 'E1' No 947, especially provided by New Cross depot, which, knowing what might happen to it, had sent a car that was due for scrapping. I would have gone to watch but for a bad cold, but Mum and Dad went and joined the hundreds outside the depot. The tram was packed with revellers who had bought special tickets, and so dense were the crowds lining the route that Stan had to 'creep along very carefully at a snail's pace', fearful of what might happen to his resistances; to help cool these he had provided an extra sack of sand and a can of water, spreading the sand out over the platform and damping it with the water. It took him an hour to get from Norbury to Telford Avenue, and by the time he pulled into the depot 'there wasn't much of the tram left. Outside the depot my wife got up on the front and gave me a kiss, then I had to throw all the people off, pick up my conductor and take the tram down to Charlton to be turned over and scrapped … I was choked, really, to think that was the last time we'd see the old trams … They had such pleasant memories for me, from a kid upwards, as you might say. I never drove a tram again.'

Above: A poignant picture, taken on the afternoon of 5 July 1952, the very last day of London's original tram network. The leading car is 'HR2' No 123, 'HR2s' and the identically bodied 'E3s' being much the largest group to survive until the very end. The trams are passing an estate of prefab homes in Plumstead High Street, which was served not only by the 36 and 38 trams routes but also the 696 and 698 trolleybuses, hence the plethora of overhead wires. The devastation wreaked upon South East London, in particular, during the Blitz and then again with the V1 and V2 attacks of 1944/5 meant that in order to rehouse families as quickly as possible temporary prefabricated homes were provided, often on cleared bombsites but sometimes on any available empty spaces; there were for instance a number on Streatham Common. Some 150,000 were built, many by German or Italian prisoners of war, often completed in a day. Intended to last no longer than 10 years, they were sometimes rather better than what their occupants had known before ('Goodness – a bathroom *and* a separate toilet!' exclaimed one), and many tenants were loath to leave them. Indeed some of the prefabs survived for decades, and one group of six, on the Excalibur Estate in Catford, is still with us today. Many groups (tenants, preservationists and those who realised what an architectural artefact they were) fought long and hard for them, and they have now been saved for posterity – as, happily, has 'HR2' tram No 1858, which regularly passed by. *A. D. Packer*

12

DEPOTS

An 'E3' outside Wandsworth depot. This building, somewhat altered,
still exists today and is used to house sightseeing buses.

Few aspects of the tram network were more intriguing, mysterious or out of bounds to the general public – and therefore higher on the list of 'must-sees' – than depots. Sadly I didn't manage to get inside one (properly, that is) until 60 years after the last tram had driven out. Said depot was Brixton Hill. I certainly got to peer inside several depots when trams were still in residence but never set foot within the portals, although I later visited a number – sometimes by invitation, sometimes not – which had once been home to trams but by then accommodated trolleybuses.

At the creation of London Transport in 1933 there were 35 depots which provided warmth, shelter and tender loving care for the London tram. By 1945 these had been reduced to 12, many of the others having converted into homes for trolleybuses. Two – Wandsworth and Holloway – housed both. Most of the rest had been disposed of, although one or two were retained for diverse purposes. Of the 12 surviving in 1945 eight are officially recorded as being converted to bus garages between 1950 and 1952, although in almost all cases the tram depot was completely demolished and a new building erected on the site; Wandsworth was the only one where substantial parts of the old depot were retained. Of these eight, Thornton Heath, Brixton Hill, Walworth, New Cross and Highgate (which was renamed Holloway in 1971, thereby causing much historical confusion) still operate buses serving various routes, whilst Wandsworth, now a Grade II Listed building, is owned by Arriva and houses buses used on the Original Sightseeing Tour. Parts of others, several going back to horse-tram days, remain extant, although their origins are not always obvious. On the plus side a brand-new depot, for Tramlink, was opened in Therapia Lane, Croydon, in November 1999.

South and west

Nearest to home, less than five minutes' walk away and near enough on quiet early mornings to hear the residents leaving for work, was Thornton Heath. Dating

Above: One could almost always be sure of encountering a stationary line of cars outside New Cross depot, the largest in London. In this scene dating from c1949 none of the Executive's employees appears too bothered. At the head of the procession is No 011, a wheel-carrier dating from 1909; it lasted until the very last day of the first generation of London trams, thereby attaining the grand age of 43 years and representing a very sound investment by the LCC. *A. W. V. Mace*

from pre-Corporation horse-car days – October 1879 to be precise – and rebuilt and enlarged in readiness for electrification in September 1901, it was Croydon Corporation's headquarters and repair facility. Its maximum capacity was 37 bogie cars. As at a number of other depots, access was gained by a single track with scarcely enough room for trams to squeeze in and out between the adjoining buildings. It was easy enough to see inside if one peered into the gloom, but, frustratingly, beyond the initially straight tracks one could see that they suddenly swung around to the left and presumably continued on whither who knows what mysteries were concealed. Actually I would probably have been rather

Above: An inspector on duty near Wandsworth depot c1949, with an 'E3' on route 12 in the background. Conduit track graces the street, the overhead wires being required by trolleybuses. Both trams and trolleybuses disappeared from Wandsworth depot on 1 October 1950.

been a wholesale redistribution of the fleet; the 'E1s' had disappeared and been replaced by a consecutively numbered batch of 'E3s', and as a consequence the streets of Croydon could boast some of the most modern cars in the London Transport fleet.

Purley was the other depot built by Croydon Corporation. This was even more intriguing, for it was situated at the far end of the 16/18 route, the furthest south of London's tram depots, its inhabitants visible only from the top deck of a passing tram – or bus. But what inhabitants. The official line was that the last trams without windscreens in normal service had either had them fitted or been withdrawn by 1940, so I had no memory of them; yet there, over the gate in Purley depot as late as 1948 were several such trams, battered, scarred, with peeling paint, not only devoid of windscreens but with broken panes elsewhere. Purley had by this time ceased to be an operating depot and was used to store redundant vehicles. In the days of my extreme youth I knew nothing of trams without windscreens and assumed that these specimens had been damaged, as had so much of my world, by enemy action during the Blitz. Which made them objects of fascinating horror. Did they contain bloodstains or even dead bodies? Such thoughts do occur to small boys brought up during a war. In fact some of them had been damaged during the war; others had been withdrawn intact but without windscreens and stored in case they might be needed in an emergency, as indeed some had been. After these had all been broken up and their remains disposed of, in the last couple of years of its existence Purley once again became an operating depot, the trams being transferred from Thornton Heath, which was demolished to make way for the replacement bus garage. By 1948 some of the conductors were women, and as there were no provision for them at the by now very outdated Purley (although women had been employed during World War 1) they had to be sent off to other depots, presumably without being given much choice.

Purley depot did not suffer the same fate as Thornton Heath, remaining intact for several decades under various owners. For a long period it housed Schweppes lorries, the vehicles (I presume) being parked over the tracks which were still *in situ*. A few yards up the Brighton Road in the Purley direction was the 'Royal Oak' public house, handy for off-duty tram crews. In 1958, seven years after the trams had gone, I had a holiday job as a labourer with a Thornton Heath building firm, and we were sent to do

disappointed, for there would simply have been more of the same, *i.e.* former Croydon Corporation 'E1s' and ex-LCCs 'E3s'. Before the conversion of route 30 to trolleybus operation in 1937 Thornton Heath had been home to a number of former LCC 'E1s', but with the transformation of the 16 and 18 routes consequent upon the arrival of the 'Felthams' at Telford Avenue there had

Above: Thornton Heath depot *c*1948, with 'E3' No 1942 on the left, a rehabilitated ex-Croydon Corporation 'E1' behind and two original ex-Croydon 'E1s', Nos 389 and 388, alongside. *D. W. K. Jones, courtesy of the National Tramway Museum ©*

Right: Purley depot *c*1946. For some years this had been used to store withdrawn and lightly war-damaged trams which might have been resuscitated if required in case of emergency, but by now they were awaiting scrapping. No 1732 was a Hurst Nelson car of 1922. Peering over the gates from the upper deck of a passing 'Feltham', the author assumed that the lack of windscreens was in every case the result of enemy action, but in fact these cars were the last surviving London trams (apart from departmental vehicles) never to have been fitted with them. *Grenville Williams*

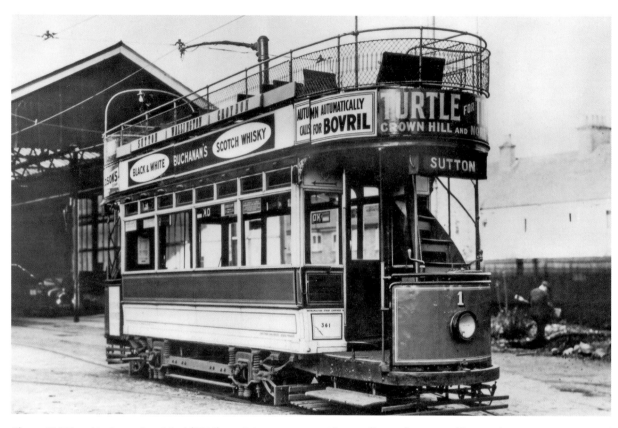

Above: SMET car No 1 seen in original (1906) condition at the company's Aurelia Road depot, which supplied trams for the West Croydon– Sutton/Mitcham routes and where in the late 1930s the more modern ex-LCC 'E' and 'E1' cars would be broken up. *Pamlin Prints*

some work at the 'Royal Oak'. Now I have no head for heights, but on my first morning I was sent up a ladder, perched precariously on the narrow pavement, and told to clear it of leaves and general gunk. Buses thundered by more or less directly beneath me – I suppose a 'Feltham' letting rip at 35mph or more might have been even scarier – as I gripped the gutter for dear life with one hand and with the other scrabbled along for the blockage. I survived, and when in future years I was sometimes faced by a class of less than wholly enthusiastic and attentive 15-year-olds I would reflect that fate could have dealt me a much worse hand career-wise.

There was a third depot within the County Borough of Croydon. This was in Aurelia Road, off the main Mitcham Road, and had been built by the South Metropolitan Electric Tramways & Lighting Co – South Met for short – when it began services between West Croydon, Mitcham and Tooting in May 1906. It was well

within walking distance of home, but I was unaware of its existence until much later, for it had not been operational since 1926. The tracks had been disconnected but in 1936 were temporarily re-connected so that large numbers of the LCC 'E' class (forerunners of the 'E1s'), which had latterly worked route 30, could be broken up upon their replacement by trolleybuses. London Transport had introduced the 'Es' and sent off the remarkably dated-looking LUT-built cars with which the route's long-suffering passengers had been saddled to the equally unfortunate patrons of the West Croydon–Sutton route, although very soon – 8 December 1935, to be precise – trolleybuses would consign them to oblivion. The route passed Croydon Aerodrome, which was, of course, London's airport, and there was more than one instance of an airliner overshooting the runway and bringing the trams to a halt – one reason why the airport had eventually to close. (Given that I have been rude about the trams it seems only fair to record that airliners of the early 1930s appeared to be made mostly of string, leftover fabric from flappers' ball gowns and motor-cycle engines; all that was about to change with the arrival of the Douglas DC-3, which had the same effect on every other airliner as had the first 'Felthams' on the rest of London's tram fleet.) The 630 trolleybus route replaced the 30 tram in September 1937. Two months later Aurelia Road depot closed, and scrapping of not just the 'Es' but also the slightly more modern and vastly more numerous 'E1s' was transferred to Purley depot, which was not now required as an operational unit; as Thornton Heath no longer had to supply trams for route 30 it was able to take over Purley's allocation on the 16, 18 and 42.

I can remember the tracks still *in situ* during the war, although I didn't know of the grimmest aspects of the Aurelia Road depot's history. When in 1944 the V1 flying bombs and later the V2 rockets were unleashed on London and particularly its southern and eastern suburbs it served as a temporary mortuary. I can still vividly recall when a V1 fell on a factory in Aurelia Road, killing large numbers of workers who were preparing to finish work. We had just returned from a holiday with Aunt Agnes and Uncle Frank, far away from the bombs, in deepest rural Shropshire: it was a sunny afternoon, we were sitting down to tea and suddenly there was the loudest explosion I had ever heard. We dashed for the Morrison shelter – a steel structure which served as a table and would protect its occupants from anything other than a direct hit – in the next room, looking up at the ceiling and fully expecting it to collapse on us, exposing the lathes I had seen so often on bomb-damaged structures. It didn't – not on that occasion. David Golfman, a member of the Building Volunteers, who had come down from Scotland, was billeted in a Nissen hut in Aurelia Road, described his experiences in a later interview. His billet 'was situated on a quadrangular compound, flanked on three sides by domestic two-storey buildings and on the other by a large, brick-built tram depot'. He moved to accommodation a short distance away and after a raid returned to the hut to find it destroyed and the occupants dead.

Brixton Hill depot is the best preserved of all those which housed the first generation of London trams, complete with its tracks and now enjoying Listed status. Next door, and of greater importance in tram days, was Telford Avenue, also known as Streatham; the boundary

Below: A line-up of 'Felthams' taking their ease in Brixton Hill depot *c*1947 before the call to duty for the evening rush-hour. From left to right are Nos 2184, 2131, 2126, 2149 and 2150. All of these would later migrate north to Leeds. *D. W. K. Jones, courtesy of the National Tramway Museum ©*

between Streatham and Brixton passed between the two depots. Telford Avenue dated from 1892, when cable cars began operating down the hill to Brixton and on to Kennington. The cable cars carried a lot of passengers but were never a match for electric ones, which were larger, heavier and much more modern. The cable cars ceased work on the night of 5 April 1904, and within a week more than a thousand men were busy carrying out the extensive conversion work. In the interim the good people of Streatham and Brixton had to make do with horse buses, and great was the rejoicing when, 11 weeks later, all was ready for the electric trams to commence a full service from Streatham Library right through to Central London. However, Telford Avenue would not be not ready for a further two years, during which time the cars working the route were accommodated at various temporary venues. When it did reopen, in March 1906, much of the cable-car building was retained, but a nod towards something rather grander was provided in the shape of an imposing Doric-arch entrance. Increasing traffic meant that an extension was soon required. This caused problems, or rather a water main at the side of the building did, and the new section, doubling the depot's capacity, had to take account of this, a footbridge being installed to enable staff to get from one half of the building to the other. The new section, on the southern (Streatham) side of the original, opened in 1912. It extended further back than did its northern neighbour, and its yard ran along the edge of a Metropolitan Board reservoir, hence the offending water main. It also sported a Doric arch, so an impression of unity was created. If not a thing of beauty then at least it had a certain presence. Each section was equipped with a traverser (standard LCC practice, Brixton Hill being the only exception), and the enlarged depot could accommodate a total of 108 bogie cars.

The only other depot which worked the Thornton Heath and Croydon routes in postwar days was Norwood. With the end of trams just over the horizon, rebuilding of Telford Avenue depot as a bus garage began in late 1949, its capacity thus being reduced, and Norwood gained some rush-hour work on the 16/18. Later, as the run-down of Telford Avenue increased, many of its trams were sent to Brixton Hill, which hitherto had had only with a limited number of rush-hour duties, and eventually, after most of the 'Felthams' had been withdrawn prior to being transferred to Leeds, it gained more and more 'E3s' and even 'E1s' from Norwood. This

was not an improvement, to put it mildly. Losing the 'Felthams' was a bitter blow, and matters were compounded by the fact that Norwood, in contrast to Thornton Heath and Telford Avenue, seemed to care little about the condition of its cars, most being shabby and unkempt. Believers in conspiracy theories, to which the author does not subscribe, claimed that this was all part of a process of softening-up the public, who would then be overjoyed when shiny, comfortable and up-to-date RTs and RTLs motor buses took over; the only problem with that was some of the RTs working the 109, the replacement for the 16/18, were less than pristine, being second-hand transfers from Wandsworth, the first depot to convert to motor buses postwar, whilst one (RT569) dated back to June 1948 and retained its 'roofbox' body. They were, nevertheless, very fine vehicles, a vast improvement over Norwood depot's shabby cast-offs.

During my research for this book I thought I had better revisit Acton tram depot, which although no tram had been seen anywhere near it since July 1936, was not only still in existence when the year 2000 dawned but wore its name proudly over its portal and was referred to as such on bus timetables. I had often passed it, especially after paying my respects at Acton depot, that treasure-trove of just about everything of importance concerning the history of transport in London from Frank Pick's armchair to 'Feltham' No 2199, so one September evening in 2011 I headed up Gunnersbury Lane and turned into the Uxbridge Road. Very odd – someone seemed to have moved it. I crossed the road, bought a Mars bar from the shop and asked the friendly proprietor where the depot had gone. 'See that block of flats they're building opposite? That's where it used to be.' How sad, I thought, for it had lasted so long that one assumed its historic importance and its rather imposing appearance had ensured it Listed status and a future; but not so. Built by LUT in 1895, it had briefly been home to horses but was soon occupied by 35 trams on seven tracks, with a track fan in the extensive forecourt. In 1936 it accommodated trams and trolleybuses together, but the trolleybuses lasted little longer than the trams, operating from there only whilst Hendon and Stonebridge Park depots were being modified. After that it served a number of purposes, including offering refuge to wagons used to repair the trolleybus overhead. Rather surprisingly it returned to operational duties in 1990 when CentreWest began operating buses from it. Its brick façade and four stone-faced arches were spruced up, 'Uxbridge Buses' and 'Acton Tram Depot' were applied boldly, and its future seemed assured. Sadly this proved not to be so, for it closed in 2008 and was then demolished. We really need to be careful in protecting our industrial buildings; many have been saved, but many others which ought to have been cherished – and perhaps, like cotton and woollen mills in Lancashire and Yorkshire, adapted for other purposes – have been lost.

A tram depot with a rather interesting – not to say chequered – history but very much still with us is Stamford Brook (not to be confused with Stamford Bridge, where you can find 22 slightly overpaid men in shorts kicking a ball, and sometimes each other, about the park and who wouldn't recognise a double-deck bus if one ran them over, unless it were an open-top one hired to give them an opportunity to display some ill-gotten trophy). It is to be found just down the road from the site of Chiswick Works and pre-dates it, as well as having outlived it by some years. Known in those days as Chiswick depot, it was erected in the early 1880s on the north side of Chiswick High Road, complete with a paddock where its 150 horses could relax on days off. The horses disappeared on 4 April 1901, the day

London's first electric tram service began, most of the horses destined, one suspects, for the knacker's yard, although some may have still had some life in them. A handsome power station was constructed of brick with stone facings, the finishing touch being two stone ladies who rejoiced in the names of 'Electricity' and 'Locomotion' and who adorned the façade. (When did you last see a statue outside a bus garage?) A new depot for the trams was erected at the same time, this consisting of two sheds capable of housing 72 bogie vehicles. The whole set-up was much admired, both for its technical and for its architectural features, as well it might, being the headquarters of LUT. The architect was the distinguished 26-year-old William Curtis Green, who later did much work in the garden town/suburbs of Letchworth and Hampstead and who also designed the Dorchester Hotel in Park Lane.

Chiswick's days of pre-eminence were short-lived, for Fulwell depot, opened two years later, assumed much of its importance; the offices were later transferred to Manor

Below: Acton Tram Depot, as it was still officially known on 1 May 2000 when used by Uxbridge Buses.

Above: Fulwell depot in 1981. Although the last tram had left some 46 years earlier the tracks remain. Beyond the employees' cars (most notably a rather fine Ford Cortina Mk3) is a line of Ms and withdrawn DMSs and SMSs.

Which brings us to Fulwell depot. Whilst not wishing to offend its inhabitants I have to say that there is little o distinguish Fulwell from a great many other fairly far-flung outer suburbs. It is looked down upon by thousands of people from all over the world, although only a handful would actually know what they were looking at, should they glance southwards, as their airliner approaches the runway at Heathrow. Fulwell consists mostly of early-20th-century semi-detached houses, many of them housing Heathrow's workers. Much the most distinguished house in the vicinity is Strawberry Hill, Horace Walpole's newly restored mid-18th-century Gothic extravaganza, a mile to the east of the depot and in sight of the Thames, whilst even nearer is Bushy Park, through which it is possible to walk to Hampton Court (which no one could ever describe as semi-detached) or Kingston, where there was once another royal palace. Fulwell-based trams and, later, trolleybuses and now motor buses, passed/pass Strawberry Hill, Hampton Court, Bushy Park and Kingston.

All of this is to prepare you for the statement that, whatever lies within Fulwell itself, its bus garage, opened in 1903 as Fulwell Tram Depot & Works, is quite possibly its finest building. To quote Robert J. Harley, in his book *United Electric Tramways* (Capital Transport, 2010)], it is 'one of the most imposing depot buildings ever erected by a London tramway operator'. Four handsome brick arches, between them spanning 135ft, form the backcloth to the extensive forecourt, which, then as now, is graced with flowerbeds – if not a lot. Throughout the trolleybus era and beyond, the forecourt was also graced with tram lines set into the cobbles, so that it was possible to find parked thereupon not only 'Diddlers', 'Q1s' and finally 'L3s' but also, in later years, Routemasters and Metrobuses; the lines have now gone. There were 15 tracks, which could accommodate 165 cars, and another three in the repair shop with room for 24 cars. Vehicles out of use, often slated for withdrawal and eventual scrapping, have always found a last resting place within its cavernous portals. By the late 1920s LUT was already breaking up some of its oldest cars; you could buy a body for £4. More than 30 years later, during the last few months of the trolleybus system, I found stored there numerous trolleybuses of various types that never actually ran in service from Fulwell, and, 20 years later still, redundant Routemasters were to be found parked outside, although many of these ultimately passed on to other owners. It is a practice that continues to this day; only recently, on alighting from my

House, while the power station became redundant in 1913 (electricity being obtained henceforth from Lots Road power station), and in 1922 it was sold to the LCC. It never served as a tram depot with London Transport, the last trams having departed in 1932, but being so near Chiswick Works it operated for some years as an overflow facility for motor buses, and in the mid-1930s newly delivered trolleybuses – routes 655, 657 and 667 passed the front door – were stored here prior to entering service. The power station was demolished in 1962, and four years later BEA's fleet of '4RF4' coaches moved in. The depot became a fully fledged bus garage in 1980, when, renamed Stamford Brook, it provided a home to exiles – men and machines (210 staff and 45 buses) – from Turnham Green, which garage's code (V) it perpetuated. Sixteen years later it closed yet again, albeit this time for only a brief period, being reactivated in October 1999 and thereafter remaining open as an operational bus garage.

267 bus (the direct successor of the 667 trolleybus route and the 67 tram) and watching it turn into the forecourt of the garage, as it now is, there to take a breather before heading back to Hammersmith, I noted a group of London United Alexander-bodied Volvos whose days as London buses were over, although no doubt they were destined for further employment in the provinces, where passengers are clearly only too grateful to be allowed a ride in the capital's cast-offs. However, Fulwell didn't just deal in the time-expired; quite the opposite, for in 1930/1 the body shells of the 'Feltham' trams, both MET and LUT examples, which were being assembled locally at the Union Construction Co's works, were taken to Fulwell, where they were completed and sent out on trial runs before taking up work, albeit never on the routes operated by Fulwell depot. It was found that the 'Felthams' were too long to work these, except in emergency; in any case these were the least profitable of LUT's routes, and the 'Felthams' natural habitat was the Uxbridge Road, on the lengthy route 7.

Some depots survived for many years after the trams and, later, the trolleybuses had departed, in the ownership of local authorities which found other uses for them, often to house various municipal vehicles. Neither Erith nor Bexley, for instance, was needed by London Transport once the trams had departed in 1935, but both lasted for some decades before eventually being demolished in the 1970s. Most spectacular of all is the hugely imposing Greenwich power station, dating from 1902, built by the LCC along the Thames and complete with a jetty where barges unloaded coal. It dwarfs its neighbour, the Trinity Hospital Almshouses of 1613,

Above: Fulwell depot in 2011. The tracks have finally been removed, but the handsome façade survives. In the foreground is a Scania bearing the initials of the modern-day London United's parent company RATP, the Parisian transport undertaking.

Below: Every bit as impressive as Fulwell is the surviving façade of Stamford Brook garage (as it is now). It had started out as Chiswick horse-tram depot in 1883, but upon electrification it was transformed by William Curtis Green, best known for the Dorchester Hotel of 1930. The depot was last used by trams in April 1932.

which, according to the plaque outside, 'since 1617 has provided a home for 21 retired gentlemen of Greenwich', although this latter, it must be admitted, probably had rather more to do with Greenwich's becoming a World Heritage Site than did either the power station or the scrapyard on its other side. The jetty is no longer in use, but the generating station still is, for which the London Underground is most grateful.

North and west

The depot which has earned itself top billing in this chapter has to be that at Nos 38/40 Upper Clapton Road, which started life on 12 July 1873 as Lea Bridge Tramway Depot. The property of the North Metropolitan Tramway Co, it housed horses and trams, was enlarged in the years 1885-7 by the LCC, and was made redundant at the time of electrification, being replaced by Hackney depot, just down the road (which itself dated from 1883), yet somehow it has survived to the present day – just. Given

local listing by Hackney Council and granted Priority Employment Site status in 2011, it provides jobs for around 100 people. This notwithstanding, Hackney's planning committee decided on 4 April 2011 to demolish most of it, despite sustained opposition led by the Hackney Society, which fought long and hard to retain it, pointing out that it was a key building, one of the few left from the very early days of Hackney, when the area was being transformed from a rural community into an industrialised London suburb. However, demolition did not follow, and when I visited in March 2012 the depot was still intact. I carefully made my way past a collection of elderly if not quite vintage cars, parked on cobbled setts between brick industrial buildings which certainly looked mid-Victorian, reached the end, where foam packing blocks and sheets were being tossed around, and was invited inside by a most obliging employee, who, in response to my enquiries, confirmed: 'Yes, there is some trackwork set into the floor – come and look.' This, of course, I did, noting also the plethora of iron columns holding up the roof – features that would be lost if redevelopment goes ahead. My guide said that as far as he knew this still on the cards but that nothing was certain.

From 1940 until April 1952 Holloway was the only tram depot north of the river. It was huge, with 26 tracks providing accommodation for no fewer than 307 trams, although even when I first knew it, in 1948, a long time had passed since anything like that number could be found in residence. I did manage a visit, but only once the trams were long gone. That was in August 1960, eight years after the last trams had departed, leaving trolleybuses in sole occupation. These had first appeared in 1938, but because the three Kingsway Subway tram routes survived the war trams and trolleys lived side by side. Amongst the latter I found were 'J3' No 1045, of the first, 1938 group of tram usurpers, and No 1538, an

'M1' of 1939, which had shared their home with trams for 12 and 11 years respectively. 'Long gone' was certainly how 1952 looked at the beginning of the Swinging Sixties; perversely, more than half a century later, it seems like only yesterday.

Just down the road Hampstead depot, which had ceased operating trams in July 1938, had nevertheless remained open, redundant trams being sent there for breaking-up. With the outbreak of war all scrapping ceased, and trams sent to Hampstead now had a future, if a limited one, being kept in reserve as potential replacements for fellow members of the tram fleet which might be destroyed in the reign of destruction that was

Below: A wonderfully esoteric collection of London Transport hardware inside Holloway depot c1950. Standing over the inspection pits are three 'E3s' which worked regularly through the Kingsway Subway, whilst to the right of them is a four-wheel works car. Just visible beyond on the far right are a couple of trolleybuses, which had been operating out of Holloway since 1938. STL1365, used to instruct tram drivers who would soon be in charge of motor buses, is lurking in the background, presumably doing its best to avoid falling into one of the pits. *London Transport*

now certain to follow. In the event, appalling though the destruction was, the total number of casualties was a relatively low 73, although hundreds more suffered damage of varying degrees of severity. With the return of peace, breaking-up resumed at Hampstead, the connection with Holloway depot being maintained each Friday by a tram keeping the tracks clear (though presumably not the same one each time). The actual scrapping was carried out by the George Cohen 600 Group, which would later deal with the trolleybus fleet. January 1947 saw Hampstead depot finally end its association with the London tram. The newly created British Road Services moved in, and scrapping was transferred first to Clapham and New Cross depots and thence to Brixton Hill and Purley. A few unlucky cars summoned to Charlton Works, no doubt expecting to re-emerge renewed and revitalised, discovered that their time was up and were broken up there, a few parts, trucks and electrical fittings surviving as spares. Incidentally, a tram overhauled post 1945 could look almost pristine in its newly applied coat of red and broken white, with no body sag and with re-upholstered

seats, prompting many to wonder if doomsday might yet be postponed or even averted altogether.

Holloway shared some routes with Finchley, another depot I visited in its final trolleybus days. A short way south of the 'Tally Ho!', a well-known tram and trolleybus junction, it was built by MET in 1905, with space for 60 cars, and later had the good fortune to be allocated the MET 'Felthams' as they were delivered. How I would love to have seen them arrive, ultra-modern, their red-and-off-white livery immaculate, putting every other form of transport to shame (although, come to think of it, a visit to the National Tramway Museum at Crich when prototype 'Feltham' No 331 is running allows one

Below: Trolleybuses inside Finchley depot in 1961. Now bright and airy, it had been transformed in 1930/1, in readiness for the 'Felthams', at a cost of £25,000. A contemporary article on its transformation spoke of an interior 'kept clean and free from mess', with the result that 'the men can work in comfortable conditions'. Little alteration was needed when the trolleybuses ousted the last trams in March 1938. The trolleybuses in turn departed in January 1962, the depot, by now Finchley bus garage, closing in December 1993.

to experience something pretty similar, particularly if some open-fronted, Edwardian-era trams are also at work, providing the sort of comparison which confronted the citizens of Middlesex in the early 1930s). In order to make them feel at home MET extended the depot and provided a traverser, whilst the generous supply of glass lights created an unusually bright and airy atmosphere. By a coincidence, just as the 'Felthams' were by far the longest production trams to work in London, so the first lengthened Routemasters, the RMLs, were delivered to Finchley to take up work on the 104 (Moorgate–Barnet) from 8 November 1961, replacing route 609's trolleybuses, which had earlier replaced the trams on route 9 (although this had been worked by Holloway depot). I once bought a Vauxhall Viva from a dealer in Finchley, which was a nice enough car except it didn't like going out in the rain – something which certainly didn't bother 'Felthams'. I have in my possession a postcard featuring two 'Felthams' splashing gaily through floods at Finchley in MET days with a Ford 8 saloon looking very apprehensive. The card was posted by my mother from Shrewsbury on 9 March 1965 – its postmark advertising the Shropshire & West Midlands Great Show two months hence – to my father in Thornton Heath. How she managed to purchase such a card so very far removed in time and distance from early-1930s Finchley is one of life's great mysteries.

Hendon was rather more than a depot, and even at the very end of the tram/ trolleybus era it served another function, that of breaking-up the vast majority of the largest trolleybus fleet in the world. Long before that, in 1910, it had been the scene of London's first trolleybus trials. In 1950 it was renamed Colindale, presumably so as not to confuse any of the prewar STDs based at Hendon bus garage, which after a particularly strenuous day working route 13 to and from the West End and the City might otherwise forgetfully have attempted to return for their cocoa and a good night's rest under the wires. Opened by MET in 1903, Hendon *depot*, aside from having four tracks for storing its trams, was also a works and a traffic-staff school, and for a period in the early 1930s it was used exclusively as a repair centre, not only for MET vehicles but for those of LUT and SMET also. Operating trams returned in 1935 but lasted for only a year or so, until replaced by trolleybuses in August 1936, although for a further three months trams continued to make their final journey to Hendon, for breaking-up. Some 23 years later trolleybuses would suffer a similar fate, George Cohen having assumed the task of disposing of the fleet, on the large plot of land behind the one-time depot. The building itself was demolished some years later.

A short distance southwest of Hendon was Stonebridge Park depot, which provided trams for routes 60, 62 and 66 and had opened in October 1906, beside what is now the North Circular Road and close to the then LNWR carriage depot on the railway line out of Euston. Its 12 roads could accommodate 48 trams, although more had to be squeezed in during the British Empire Exhibition in 1924/5, and in 1936 it was enlarged to accommodate trolleybuses. I paid my one and only visit on its last day as a trolleybus depot, 2 January 1962, when some of the heaviest snow to which the suburbs had been subjected for many years provided some rather splendid photographic opportunities, although these were appreciated neither by drivers manœuvring their six-wheel mammoths through slush and melting snow nor passengers stamping hands and feet as they waited miserably for the trolleys to struggle through; the extensive forecourt of the depot was solid white, here and there turning a delicate shade of muddy brown. Motor buses took the place of the trolleys, remaining until Stonebridge *garage*, as it had become, closed in the summer of 1981.

13

WHAT'S LEFT

Carlton Colville recreates bygone London with 'HR2' tram No 1858, a 1938-vintage Austin taxi and two trolleybuses, 'C2' No 260 and 'K2' No 1201.

A fair amount of London's original tram system survives, ranging from trams themselves to some very minor artefacts which have survived purely by chance but which, in the manner of a world which places more and more emphasis on preserving the past, are now considered worth saving. In the latter category are a couple of loops fixed into the rear wall of Brixton Hill depot to which were once attached the overhead power lines. At the other extreme is the depot itself. It was originally intended to house the trailer cars which came into use in 1913 and which proved their worth during World War 1, but these gradually fell out of use, partly because they slowed services down and partly because a further influx postwar of higher-powered 'E1s' had rendered them obsolete, and the last ceased working on the Brixton routes at the end of 1922. The depot did not open until 1924 and so was used as an overflow for electric cars from Telford Avenue, mainly working the morning and evening peaks. Although Telford Avenue depot was demolished and replaced by a bus garage in 1951, Brixton Hill depot survived and, still owned by London Transport, eventually became a car showroom. Although cars were usually parked outside it was possible to detect the rails laid in stone setts. One afternoon in 2005, looking down from the upper deck of a Routemaster working the 159, I noticed these being replaced, this being a prelude to Arriva's taking over the premises as bus travel in London grew and Brixton *garage* (in Telford Avenue) found it could no longer house all the buses it was required to operate. Today the former tram depot is used mainly by buses working peak-hour services, history thus repeating itself. Within the depot the tracks, of which there are seven, remain (with a short stub, about one tramcar's length, projecting from one), these coming together by the entrance. Such is Arriva's appreciation of the its inheritance that their future is assured. Other depots (or parts thereof) also survive, as we have already seen, but Brixton Hill is unique in that it is so little changed from when trams lived there.

The best known and most visible section of surviving track is that leading down into the Bloomsbury end of the Kingsway Subway, double track laid in stone setts and protected by metal gates. Track survived elsewhere for decades after the trams themselves had gone, notably in Beresford Square, Woolwich, and on the forecourt of Fulwell depot, and there are certainly other examples still *in situ* but covered with tarmac. When Tramlink tracks were being laid, and George Street, Croydon, was

Above: Brixton Hill depot in May 2012, now a Listed building and used by Arriva, two of whose employees are prominent. The buses normally housed here are out and about on rush-hour duties.

being excavated, some of the original rails, over which trams had last passed in 1927, were discovered, and doubtless there are many similar relics waiting to be unearthed all over London. Apart from the preserved trams themselves, of which more anon, the model world is also doing a sterling job in keep alive the memory of London's trams. The only mass-produced model of fairly recent times – and one which captures very successfully the lines of the original – is the Corgi 1:72-scale OO-gauge 'Feltham'. This has been produced in several liveries, although, curiously, none in its postwar guise working from Telford Avenue depot on the 16/18 route, which is how many of us would remember it – and, one would have thought, a likely best-seller. It can also be motorised. There have been several kits to the same gauge, a long-lived one being the Tower Trams 'E1'. This is a plastic kit, requiring a fair degree of skill to do a good job, but is certainly worth it, whether without a windscreen (which is a bit easier) or with one. Both are in London Transport guise. Tower Trams also produces the 'Feltham' in various forms. As yet no-one has brought out a kit of a London tram along the lines of modern bus and coach (and, indeed, London trolleybus) kits, whereby the body, seats etc are all pre-formed and which are therefore much easier for someone, like your author, who rather lacks the patience and skill for the fiddly older-style kits. When one considers what an amazing proliferation of bus models there has been of late (some of them, let it be said, of pretty obscure prototypes) it is surprising that no-one – despite a few heavy hints from your author – has considered an 'E3'/'HR2' as a commercial proposition.

There are some very fine, etched-brass kits by Chris Cornell, which are suitable for motorisation and require quite a bit of skill, and there are some wonderful working layouts, often with scratch-built trams, which can be seen at various events. The mecca for tram enthusiasts is the annual Festival of Model Tramways, now in its 24th year and held at a variety of venues including Crich and, in London, at the Kew Bridge Steam Museum. But there are many others, and for London enthusiasts the regular model-themed events held at Acton Museum are a must. One layout which has appeared there and which appeals greatly to your author is that of Colin Withey (who knows more about Croydon trams than most people have forgotten) and others, which represents the area around West Croydon, both prior to 1951 and in the modern Tramlink era. A delightful O-gauge layout is 'Cheerio Charlton', by Richard Mowles, whilst two 1:16-scale ones, by John Prentice, feature East Ham in the early 1930s and the Aldgate/Whitechapel area in 1934 – which, as John explains, marks the zenith of the London tram, being the year before conversion to trolleybuses began, and when the variety of types was at its greatest. Another very fine 1:16-scale layout is that of the Sussex Area of the Tramway & Light Railway Society, founded way back in 1938. When I visited Acton in March 2012 working examples of an ex-Croydon four-wheeler, an MET 'Ally Pally' single-decker, an 'E1', a prototype 'Feltham', No 1 and a Tramlink car, amongst others, were on display.

Bursting on the scene since the dawn of the 21st century has been John Howe, who, although he was born after the last of the first generation of London trams had vanished, has done as much as anyone to recreate those days. Under the trade name of Kingsway he has produced a range of card-kit bus garages and tram

Above Left: The southern end of the Kingsway Subway has been adapted for road traffic, which enters from Waterloo Bridge, but the remaining, northern section is little changed, with tram tracks still in place, and has served a variety of functions, not least as a valuable resource for film-makers. This is the Bloomsbury approach today.

Left: Close by the erstwhile Subway is the disused Aldwych station on the Central Line. This had opened in 1907 as 'Strand', being renamed in 1915; closed during World War 2, it reopened in 1946 and finally closed again in 1994. It too has often used by film-makers, and occasionally parties of the general public are allowed down. This photograph was taken early in 2012.

Above: A meeting which certainly never happened in reality but which the model world is able to create: Croydon Tramlink No 2530 in its original livery and No 552, one of the final batch of LCC 'E1s' of 1930.

Left: A fine working model of No 320, seen at an open day at Acton Museum. Next to it is No 1, whilst beyond are preserved full-size buses, among them a Red Arrow 'Merlin' and an RF.

depots and exhibits two extensive OO-gauge working layouts, of Dog Kennel Hill in Dulwich, with its four-track section, and the Kingsway Subway, using a mixture of scratch-built models and modified Corgi 'Felthams' and Tower Trams 'E1s'.

So what of full-size survivors? In a minute, in a minute, but first we must travel to south Devon, where a narrow-gauge tramway operates on the trackbed of a former LSWR branch line to Seaton. Amongst its fleet is No 12, a much-rebuilt tram which in its present incarnation (dating from 1999) resembles an open-top 'Feltham', albeit with a somewhat reduced seating capacity when compared to the real thing. Then there is No 2, which is based on an MET 'A' type but was actually built when the tramway was based at Eastbourne, in 1964. Much the most interesting of the trio of London-style trams to be found at Seaton is No 14, which really did start life as a Metropolitan 'A' type – No 94, in 1905 – and after serving as a holiday home was eventually rescued and, much modified but with its very grand, ornate lower-deck interior restored, reappeared in 1984 as a single-decker.

Now for actual *bone fide* (more or less) survivors. London Transport was always aware of its duty to posterity, and when the various ancient, ex-corporation four-wheelers were being taken out of service as quickly as possible in the mid-1930s it made a point of preserving a representative, selecting the former West Ham No 102. Built by UEC in 1910 at a cost of £529, it was rebuilt in the Corporation's workshops and was actually one of the very last four-wheelers to operate in London, not being withdrawn until 1938. Originally restored as London Transport No 290, it was later and most properly put back into West Ham livery and at the time of writing is the only electric tram on display at Covent Garden. It was inevitable that a member of the 1,000-strong 'E1' type would be chosen to represent the standard London tram when the postwar conversion of tram to motor buses got underway, and in January 1952 No 1025, instead of heading for a fiery end at the Penhall Road, Charlton, scrapyard, found itself being towed to the Country Area garage at Reigate to join various other lucky representatives of London's bygone public transport. No-one now seems to be able to recall why No

1025, of 1907 vintage, was singled out, but it may be because it was one of only 50 of its type to have an LCC-built body; that the upper deck retained low, wooden-back seats was possibly another reason. One other tram was preserved at this time, this being ex-LCC 'HR2' No 1858, which was taken out of service in July 1952 and sold to a private collector. At that time my father worked at the NAAFI headquarters at Ruxley Towers, which was, most handily, near Chessington Zoo, where No 1858 was put on display, so I used to see it regularly. It was later moved to the East Anglia Transport Museum at Carlton Colville, near Lowestoft, where, restored to working order, it has for decades been one of the very few original London trams upon which it is still possible to ride.

Nearly all tramway systems converted elderly trams into service or engineering vehicles, and London had quite a fleet of these. They were a familiar part of the tramway scene, albeit one I largely ignored; shame on me, for I should have realised that they took us back to the very beginning of London's electric trams, being the only examples that I can recall seeing on which the driver was still exposed to the full force of whatever the elements decided to throw at him. One such was No 022, a snowbroom. This had begun life as 'B'-class car No 106, a four-wheeler dating from 1903, with open-top double-deck bodywork by the Electric Railway & Carriage Co. Although modified over the years the 'Bs' were disposed of quite quickly, and our No 106 was converted to a snowbroom in the mid-1920s. Richard Elliott, a staff member of the National Museum of Transport, situated on the site of the former Clapham tram depot, had been a tramway engineer at Charlton Works, and he it was who realised how valuable a relic No 022 was. Although the museum had hoped to restore it (and had acquired a number of parts from other cars), this proved impracticable, and the tram was placed in the care of the London County Council Tramways Trust, which began the task of restoration. This was eventually completed, and today one can ride on No 106 at the National Tram Museum at Crich.

But surely, you must be thinking, London would have preserved one of the legendary 'Felthams'? Not straightaway, for the simple reason that almost the entire fleet was sold to Leeds for further service. Two were damaged before they could make the journey north, so No 1 was offered in lieu, and that too took itself off to Yorkshire. As a second-year art student, demobbed from the

Above left: A Corgi model 'Feltham' emerges from the Kingsway model of Brixton Hill depot.

Left: The interior of Seaton Tramway No 14. This was originally MET 'A'-class car No 94, built in 1904 and converted between 1962 and 1984 to its present narrow-gauge, single-deck form.

Right: LCC No 106 in all its preserved glory at Crich. Built by Dick, Kerr & Co in 1903 to serve the (then) less-demanding South East London routes, the four-wheel 'B'-class cars were gradually replaced by higher-capacity bogie cars, some being sold, while in the mid-1920s no fewer than 20 were converted to snowbrooms, among them No 106, which was renumbered 022. However, with the final abandonment of the trams in the years 1950-2 its historical importance was recognised, and eventually a start was made on its restoration. It had begun life operating on the conduit system, but as there was no likelihood of its being able to run thus in preservation the decision was taken to restore it to the condition in which it had been altered in 1908 to work under the overhead between Plumstead and Woolwich – a task that was finally completed by the LCC Tramways Trust in 1982.

Below right: LCC No 106 boldly invites South East Londoners to sample the delights of Abbey Wood.

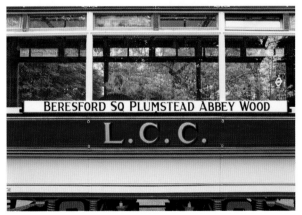

RAF, I hitch-hiked to Leeds in the summer of 1960, hoping to renew my friendship with the 'Felthams', only to discover that trams had ceased to operate in that city the previous year. 'Feltham' No 2155, originally MET No 355, was brought back to become part of the London Transport Collection and regained MET livery. No 2085 emigrated to the USA, taking up residence the Seashore Trolley Museum at Kennebunkport, Maine, whilst a third remained in Leeds, on the Middleton Railway, but after being vandalised was eventually scrapped. A fourth 'Feltham' to survive beyond 1952 was one of the experimental cars, the centre-entrance No 331 of 1930, which, because it could not be fitted with conduit pick-up apparatus, was sold in 1937 to Sunderland Corporation. This system closed in 1954, and No 331 was acquired by preservationists, ended up at Crich. It was eventually restored to working order for the Gateshead Garden Festival of 1990 and, now back in London livery, serves as a wonderful reminder of just how luxurious and how far ahead of its time the 'Feltham' was. After service in Leeds No 1 also passed to the Tramway Museum Society at Crich. Repainted in London Transport livery, it has been on static display ever since,

never having run as far as I know, although funds are now being raised to allow it to be returned to passenger-carrying service.

A number of tram bodies were sold off for use as chalets, notably on Hayling Island. One such was that belonging No 1622, an 'E1' that had been taken out of service in August 1946, which became a holiday home. The lower saloon was discovered in 1970 and was eventually rescued, together with an upper saloon, and the two sections brought were to London and reunited. As a standard 'E1' had already been preserved, the decision was taken to restore No 1622 as one of the rehabilitated cars, and this was eventually done, to an extraordinarily high standard, making it another London tram on which one can ride at Crich.

That, however, is not all. There was a time when unless a vehicle was complete and in almost pristine condition it would not have been considered for preservation, but today, long after many irreplaceable trams are thought to have vanished, remains are still being unearthed, lurking in some remote farmyard or buried in a hedgerow, and painstakingly brought back to life. One such was LUT No 159, a 'W'-type car built by G. F. Milnes in 1902. Withdrawn in the 1920s, it was discovered in use as living accommodation at Ewhurst

Green, Surrey, in 1978. Once again the LCC Tramways Trust stepped in, acquiring what remained of No 159 as well as further parts, which were transported to Crich, where on 7 July 2012 I had the pleasure of attending the tram's launch in passenger traffic. Who would have thought on the night of 5/6 July 1952, when the last London tram ran into the scrapyard at Penhall Road, that 60 years later it would be possible to watch four working London trams, ranging from No 159, through an LCC four-wheel open-top car of 1903 and a rehabilitated 'E1' to a prototype 'Feltham', lined up high on a hillside in rural Derbyshire?

In the interests of research and in preparation for this book I did the noble thing and talked myself into visiting both Crich and Carlton Colville in order to travel once again upon the only two surviving traditional London

trams, 'E1' No 1622 and 'HR2' No 1858, which offer this experience. Both date from the early 1930s, by which time No 1 and the 'Felthams' were already offering a startlingly different approach to street railways. One is immediately struck by how bright are the interiors, with high, wide windows, both upstairs and down. The seats on the lower deck are attractively upholstered and comfortable, arranged two-plus-one so the that gangway is wide enough for an alighting passenger to squeeze past a standing one, although average girth has increased noticeably since 1952. Upstairs the seats are rather more basic, their upholstery designed with the effects of decades of tobacco smoke in mind. The slatted wooden floors of the 'HR2' were not merely built both also to entrap large quantities of dust, the metal-covered ones of the rehabilitated 'E1' being much smoother. The interiors of both are greatly superior to those of the original 'E1', No 1025, with its slatted wood ceilings, plethora of protruding wooden fittings, knobs and handles and low-back wooden upper-deck seats. Nos 1662 and 1858 make all the right growly, clackety noises as they spring into action, riding smoothly enough, their body framings tight and well maintained, with surprisingly few creaks and rattles. But both lack a certain refinement, with various fittings placed to suit engineers rather than accord with the wishes of an interior designer, who clearly started with a clean sheet when starting work on No 1 and the 'Felthams'.

Opposite: No 331, the experimental centre-entrance 'Feltham' of 1930, which was sold to Sunderland in January 1937. When that town's trams ceased running it was bought for preservation, being seen here, wonderfully restored to original condition, at work at the National Tramway Museum, Crich.

Top right: The view down one of No 331's central staircases, showing the conductor standing ready to supervise loading and unloading – one of the reasons MET stipulated this arrangement – and the handsome panelling lining the sides of the car.

Right: The view ahead as No 331 negotiates interlaced track at Crich.

Above: London Transport-rehabilitated 'E1' No 1622 and MET centre-entrance 'Feltham' No 331 at Glory Mine, Crich, on 7 July 2012. Although 'Felthams' and 'E1s' worked the same routes for many years (the 16 and 18 immediately spring to mind), if these two cars ever met in London their encounter would have been fleeting: the first 'rehabs' emerged in the spring of 1934, and the 'Feltham' was sold to Sunderland in January 1937.

Left: One of a number of trams bodies which retired to the country was that of No 234, which had started life in Edwardian times as West Ham Corporation No 49. A G. F. Milnes-bodied open-top four-wheeler, it was fitted with a top cover in the early 1920s, but both upper- and lower-deck ends were left exposed to the elements. London Transport initially numbered it 257 but renumbered it when the original 234 was scrapped, although as this occurred in 1934 and the entire class of 48 cars had all gone by 1937 one wonders just why they bothered.

Above: LUT No 159 about to make its first full passenger carrying journey for many decades at the National Tram Museum, Crich, on 7 July 2012. Painstakingly restored (although much of it, inevitably, is new build), it looks quite glorious, a wonderful re-creation of how this then state-of-the-art vehicle must have impressed the inhabitants of Thames-side West London when placed in service in the second year of King Edward Vll's reign.

Top right: Looking down, literally but certainly not pejoratively, on London United 'W'-type No 159 of 1902 on its first day in service at Crich, 7 July 2012 – 110 years after its very first run in West London.

Right: A line-up of four very different London trams on the occasion of the entry (or, rather, re-entry) into traffic of LUT 'W' type No 159 at Crich on 7 July 2012. The other three cars are LCC No 106 of 1903, rehabilitated 'E1' No 1622 and 'Feltham' No 331. Only No 1, which, sadly, was not brought out from under cover, is required to complete the set.

14

A NEW DAWN

No 2553 pauses beside West Croydon bus station on its way to New Addington on
19 September 2007 whilst Arriva VDL/Wright DW47 sets off for Tooting on route 264, which
serves a partial replacement for the 630 trolleybus and, before that, the 30 tram.

I still sometimes rub my eyes with disbelief as I watch a tram make its way along George Street and down Crown Hill, Croydon. If ever a sign is needed that God is still in his Heaven, that if you wish hard enough the impossible might just happen, and that what has seemingly gone for ever may well come round again if you are patient enough, then stand by the Whitgift almshouses and you too will become a believer. As I set off for school on the second Monday of April 1951 and watched no fewer than three fully laden RTs pass disdainfully by my request stop (whereas until then it had never once crossed my mind that there would not be room for me on the next 16, 18 or 42 tram) I, in common, no doubt, with many other citizens of the County Borough of Croydon, was starkly reminded that our trams had

Above: Those who had faith in trams, few though they may have been 65 years ago, were finally let back into the promised land, and today trams once again serve East Croydon and Addiscombe. Tramlink twins Nos 2549 and 2550 in their original livery of red and broken white stand outside East Croydon station in 2002.

vanished for ever. Yet there were those who, misguided though they were considered by almost everyone at the time, refused to accept the inevitable. Clinging to the faith, badgering the powers that were and the powers that weren't, producing evidence that the tram was *not* the prime cause of traffic congestion; pointing beyond our shores to numerous European cities (notably in Switzerland and Germany but also, in complete contrast, in Eastern Europe and the USSR) where the tram was still in favour, to the increasing pollution caused by the ever-growing number of private cars and to the advantages of combining under-used but potentially viable 'heavy' rail routes with reserved street running, they slowly persuaded people to start thinking the unthinkable.

In the 1950s and '60s the skyline of Croydon changed dramatically as many businesses moved out of Central London and erected high-rise offices – hence its nickname, 'Little Manhattan' (although 'The Windy City' or 'Little Chicago' would surely have be more appropriate, on account of the icy blasts which are channelled between the mini-skyscrapers) – on the much cheaper land eight miles south of Charing Cross but only a few minutes from Central London by fast train services from East Croydon station. At Christmastime in 1964 I worked for the Post Office, as did so many students in those days,

delivering parcels with a regular postman and a trainee priest, the latter having once a town planner and who proudly reminded us, each time we headed through the Park Lane underpass that he had helped design this modern wonder, prompting the thought that rather more than one underpass was by now needed to deal with the increasing pollution and traffic congestion, and not just in Croydon town centre, whilst those unfortunates banished to the huge council estate on the windy heights of New Addington ('Little Siberia') complained bitterly about the lack of decent, fast communications with the town centre, whence so many had come.

When Glasgow got rid of its last tram in 1962 the UK's first street tram service, between Blackpool and Fleetwood, became also its last. This had established itself as such an integral part of the Blackpool scene, especially during the autumn Illuminations, that its future seemed secure, but it continued in isolated splendour. However, light rail – something between a

Above: The view up Crown Hill, with the 'threepenny bit' office block alongside East Croydon station in the distance, before the days of Tramlink, in December 1991.

tramway and a suburban rail system – was slowly gaining in favour. Those who kept the faith and yet hardly dared revealed their (to others) heretical thoughts could now, cautiously, raise their heads above the parapet. One such was John Gent.

As a young National Serviceman John had managed to get leave to take part in the final day of trams in Croydon, 7 April 1951. After joining London Transport as a clerk the following year he gradually rose through the ranks and by 1974 as Principal Planning Assistant he had attended a course at the British Transport Staff College and produced a project which involved converting several railway lines around Croydon to light rail and building a new line to New Addington; he was, however, told by his boss to keep this to himself, as at that time London Transport favoured underground connections. By 1980 John was Planning Liaison Officer. Times and attitudes were now changing, and he became involved in various joint projects with British Rail, the result of which was a report, 'Light Rail for London?', which led to both the Docklands Light Railway and Croydon Tramlink. There was still a powerful lobby which wanted to put light rail underground, but John and others knew that one of the great attractions of street railways is their visibility and easy access. John retired in 1990 but wrote that to one of his team, Scott Macintosh, 'we owe a debt of gratitude for [Tramlink's] eventual completion'. He also paid tribute to Dennis Coombes of Croydon; 'Again we must be grateful for his efforts to bring

Tramlink into being.' John Gent was, like many in transport management, a dedicated enthusiast and historian. He died in 2011, but his unique collection of photographs and material related to transport in Croydon and London in general survives in the care of Croydon Library.

Another who kept the faith was Colin Withey. As a schoolboy at Gonville Primary School, even before the disappearance of Croydon's trams he had taken part in a project advocating upgrading the tram network, which had caught the eye of none other than the Mayor. Colin refused to believe that the tram would not again have its day and was involved from the very earliest days of Tramlink; he probably knows more about every aspect of Croydon trams, past and present, than does any other living soul.

The first of the new generation of light-rail/tram systems was the Tyne & Wear Metro, which opened in 1980. July 1987 saw the opening of the first section of the Docklands Light Railway, which, although none of it runs on streets, abounds with tramway-type curves, whilst its first vehicles, becoming obsolete but far from worn-out some 15 years later, were returned to Germany (where that been built) and, following modifications, took up street running in Essen. The first true new tramway to come to fruition in the UK was Manchester Metrolink, in 1992.

Parliament approved a bill for Croydon Tramlink in late 1996, and on 25 November 1996 construction work began. Completion was scheduled for November 1999. There was

Above: A pair of the original Docklands two-car units opposite the Millennium Dome, Greenwich (now O2), in the year 2000. They would later be sold to Essen, Germany, where they now run as street trams.

some vociferous, ill-informed opposition, but the vast majority of the population approved, although inevitably there were plenty of grumbles as work got underway and road works and traffic diversions proliferated.

Almost half the network was planned to make use of former railway routes, either still intact or abandoned, the rest being street running. The system would cover 28km, just under 52 track kilometres. The most westerly terminus would be at Wimbledon – not beside the Town Hall, where I used to watch the ancient 'E1s' which worked routes 2 and 4 reversing and heading back to the Embankment, but more or less beneath it, in the main-line station, where, uniquely, it would be possible to observe main-line trains, Underground trains and trams at one and the same time at different platform faces. The other Tramlink termini would be at Elmers End and Beckenham Junction stations and at New Addington.

It was probably the inhabitants of New Addington for whom Tramlink would be the biggest boon; never previously adequately linked to Croydon town centre,

Above: A poster displayed in George Street, Croydon, in September 1997, heralding the advent of Tramlink.

Below: Map of the proposed Tramlink network.

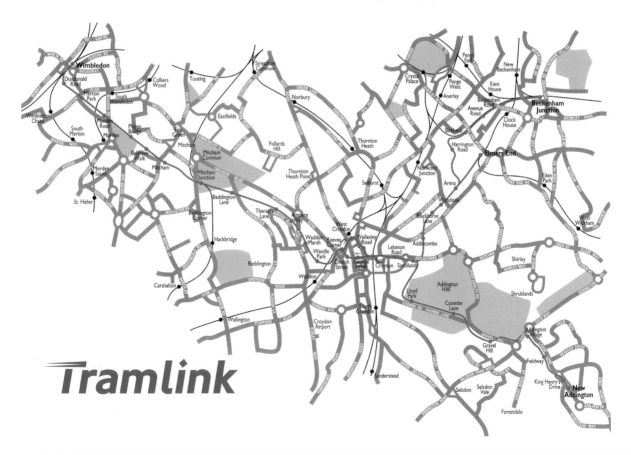

Above: Dundonald Road, Wimbledon, in April 1999, with the conversion from 'heavy' rail almost complete.

the area would at last have a fast rail route which would transform the journey. It had been intended prewar as a 'Garden Village', but neither gardens nor village ever figured prominently, and most homes were council-owned, often inhabited by families who would rather not have been there. It has had a mixed press over the years, much of it not very favourable. Quite recently Tesco closed, to be replaced by Lidl, which tells us quite a lot about what is now really a town in its own right, of some 21,000 residents. Almost all agree that quite the best thing which has ever happened to it was Tramlink, which again tells us something.

Tramlink established a depot at Therapia Lane, on the Wimbledon branch between the site of the old Croydon power station and gasworks and the southern edge of Mitcham Common. This section, incidentally, runs more or less along the trackbed of the Surrey Iron Railway, which lays claim to having been the oldest public railway in the world.

Right: Waddon Marsh station in 1961, with a Southern Region '2-EPB' two-coach electric unit working from West Croydon to Wimbledon.

The aspect which probably most intrigued enthusiasts was the type of tram Tramlink would favour. Hong Kong is the only system worldwide which has continued to specify double-deck cars, so no-one was expecting a late-20th-century version of the 'Feltham'. No two of any of the present-day British and Irish tram systems have opted for identical vehicles, and Croydon has proved no exception to this rule. However, Tramlink *did* decide upon a well-proven design, that which Bombardier had supplied to

Cologne in 1995. Twenty-four trams were ordered, articulated in three sections, with an overall length of 30.1m, a seating capacity of 70 and room for 138 standing passengers. Almost fully wheelchair-accessible, the first tram, built in Vienna, arrived at Therapia Lane on the evening of 14 September 1998. Trams were back in Croydon! Not only were they back, but they were painted in a red and white livery virtually identical to that worn by their London Transport predecessors. On top of this the tram which reached Croydon that September evening was numbered 2530; the highest-numbered first-generation tram had been 2529. Time and again I come across managers and operators of British transport systems who are not only dedicated but are true, dyed-in-the-wool transport enthusiasts, so we should not be surprised at this recognition of tradition.

By June 1999 all 24 trams had arrived, and trial running began. On 10 May 2000 the first service, between Wimbledon and New Addington, began, to be followed 13 days later by the Beckenham Junction route and finally, on 29 May, that to Elmers End. It was predicted that by the end of the first 18 months some 20 million passengers would have been carried, but within eight months growth was up by some 50% over predictions, and soon Tramlink was the busiest tram network in the UK. The trams ride beautifully. The most attractive stretch of line is that from Lloyd Park climbing up to Shirley Hills; from there, reaching a maximum of 50mph, trams speed down to the picturesque village of Addington, where an interchange has been built to accommodate various feeder bus routes and from where the trams climb alongside Gravel Hill to slightly less picturesque New Addington.

There have been a number of extension proposals, including one to reinstate trams along the route of the old 16/18 from Croydon into Central London, but the two which seem most likely (indeed Mayor of London Boris Johnson has given them his support) are those to Crystal Palace and to Sutton town centre. In October 2008 refurbishment of the trams began, with a new livery of blue, pale grey and green 'to distinguish them from local buses' – surely the oddest reason for a repaint yet heard, although it probably served its purpose inasmuch as customers were heard to comment favourably on 'the new trams'. Increasing patronage resulted in a £16 million order for six new Variobahn trams from Stadler Rail, similar to those supplied to Bergen, Norway, and these entered service in 2012. I think we can safely say that trams in Croydon are here to stay.

Below: A Bombardier K4000 tram, the prototype for Bombardier's Croydon trams, crosses the River Rhine in Cologne in 2005.

Above: Newly delivered trams inside a not-quite-completed Therapia Lane depot, 26 June 1999.

Left: No 2544 winds its way along Church Street, with Croydon Minster towering over the shops.

Below: Passengers waiting at Addington Village for the tram to take them up the hill to New Addington, July 2011.

Left: Tram No 2542 in yellow advertising livery speeds towards the summit of the line at Shirley Hills on its way to New Addington, January 2002.

Below: No 2532 below Lloyd Park, on the trackbed of the former BR Selsdon–Elmers End branch, in the summer of 2008. Just visible are another tram bound for New Addington and the portal of the tunnel from which it has just emerged.

Above: No 2533 accelerates away from Waddon towards Wimbledon, passing the two chimneys which were once part of Croydon 'B' power station and are now a feature of the IKEA store.

Opposite right: The same location in 1969, with a BR Class 33 diesel-electric locomotive, No D6512, which has just brought in a coal train, and, in the distance, a Peckett 0-4-0ST shunting coal wagons at the power station.

Opposite top: Among the advantages trams enjoy over trains are that can climb more easily and negotiate sharper bends. Here, in November 2010, a tram has passed over the West Croydon–Sutton railway line and is about to make a curving descent to Wandle Park before heading for Mitcham Junction and Wimbledon.

Opposite far right: A Wimbledon-bound tram heads over the Southern line to Dorking and Horsham before descending to the shared Mitcham Junction station in May 2002.

Above: The original West Croydon–Wimbledon railway line, single for much of its length, was a real backwater, passing through some surprisingly rural parts of outer suburbia. Some of this has been built over of late, but the section beside the River Wandle and alongside the grounds of Morden Park remains, as can be seen in this picture of No 2541 heading eastwards in May 2009, untouched by encroaching bricks and mortar.

Opposite top: A few hundred yards to the west Tramlink passes over the Northern Line, which then emerges from what was once the longest Underground railway tunnel in the world, at Morden, as seen here in 2010.

Opposite bottom: The long-closed station at Merton Park stands derelict in October 2000 as tram No 2551 passes.

Above: A tram emerges from George Street, Croydon, and prepares to descend Crown Hill, November 2010.

Right: No 2538 descends Crown Hill, September 2011.

Left: Croydon suffered particularly badly in the riots which afflicted certain towns and cities in England in August 2011. The total destruction of the long-established family-owned Reeves furniture shop at the end of Church Street, a location popularly known as Reeves Corner, attracted worldwide attention. This was the scene as a fireman, standing on the tram track, damped down the remains the next morning.

Above: Tram services resumed commendably soon afterwards, and here No 2541 passes by the now boarded-up site a few weeks later. The windows of the buildings across the street bear testimony to the ferocity of the blaze, but Reeves was already back in business, having taken over premises a block away.

Right: Newly delivered Stadler tram No 2555 on a training run in Church Street, Croydon, 22 May 2012.

BIBLIOGRAPHY

Books

Croydon Tramways by Robert J. Harley
    (Capital Transport, 2004)
LCC Electric Tramways by Robert J. Harley
    (Capital Transport, 2002)
London County Council Tramways Handbook
    (Tramway & Light Railway Society, 1970)
London Transport Tramways 1933-1952 by
    E. R. Oakley and C. E. Holland
    (London Tramways History Group, 1998)
London United Electric Tramways by Robert J. Harley
    (Capital Transport, 2010)
North London Trams by Robert J. Harley
    (Capital Transport, 2008)
The Tramways of Croydon by G. E. Baddeley
    (Light Rail Transit Association, 1983)
The Wheels Used to Talk to Us edited by
    Terence Cooper (Tallis Publishing, 1977)

Magazines

TOT / Pennyfare / London Transport Magazine (various editions)

Newspapers

Croydon Advertiser (various editions)

Other

Various documents in the possession of the late John Gent and Colin Read

Below: Tramlink – the modern face of trams in London. No 2549 descends Crown Hill, Croydon, in September 2011.